Stuart Hall

THE CARIBBEAN BIOGRAPHY SERIES

The Caribbean Biography Series from the University of the West Indies Press celebrates and memorializes the architects of Caribbean culture. The series aims to introduce general readers to those individuals who have made sterling contributions to the region in their chosen field – literature, the arts, politics, sports – and are the shapers and bearers of Caribbean identity.

Other Titles in This Series

Earl Lovelace, by Funso Aiyejina
Derek Walcott, by Edward Baugh
Marcus Garvey, by Rupert Lewis
Beryl McBurnie, by Judy Raymond
Una Marson, by Lisa Tomlinson

STUART HALL

Annie Paul

The University of the West Indies Press
Jamaica • Barbados • Trinidad and Tobago

The University of the West Indies Press
7A Gibraltar Hall Road, Mona
Kingston 7, Jamaica
www.uwipress.com

A catalogue record of this book is
available from the National Library of Jamaica.

ISBN: 978-976-640-788-9 (cloth)
978-976-640-789-6 (paper)
978-976-640-790-2 (Kindle)
978-976-640-791-9 (ePub)

Cover photograph of Stuart Hall courtesy of Clinton Hutton.

Jacket and book design by Robert Harris
Set in Whitman 11.5/15

Printed in the United States of America

For Varun

CONTENTS

ONE

It has been the main function of national cultures, which are systems of representation, to represent what is in fact the ethnic hodgepodge of modern nationality as the primordial unity of "one people". . . . What's more, this hybridity of the modern nation state is, in the present phase of globalization, being compounded by one of the largest forced and unforced mass migrations in recent times. So that, one after another, western nation states, already "diaspora-ised" beyond repair, are becoming inextricably multicultural – mixed ethnically, religiously, culturally and linguistically.

—Stuart Hall, "Our Mongrel Selves"[1]

Thus wrote Stuart Hall in the early 1990s, the most globally influential intellectual Jamaica has yet produced, skilfully unravelling the complex processes by which national identity is constituted and reconstituted in the face of rapid globalization. Identity, whether communal or individual, and the politics of who we think we are and how and why we become ourselves were the abiding focus of Hall's life and work.

He was known primarily for his pioneering work in the field of cultural studies, a disruptive new technology of scholarly inquiry that turned traditional disciplinary models of knowledge production upside down and introduced interdisciplinary work to the British academy in the 1970s. By the time he died in 2014, Hall's ideas and methods of conjunctural analysis had made inroads all over the world.

"Was this the man that launch'd a thousand dissertations? And then ten thousand more?" read a tweet lamenting Hall's death on 10 February 2014. He was always looking beyond the surface to the submerged and subcutaneous layers of reality, and another invaluable, now commonsensical, contribution made by Hall was that while the media are widely believed to reflect reality, they are, in fact, complicit in constructing it. Hall famously made this apparent in his landmark 1978 book *Policing the Crisis*, an adept analysis of the phenomenon of "Thatcherism", studying how power coopts the culture of the people – popular culture – in furthering and consolidating itself.

The innovative theoretical work Hall produced placed him on a par with other great intellectuals from the Caribbean such as Frantz Fanon, C.L.R. James, Sylvia Wynter and Edouard Glissant, while on the global stage he ranked in importance and influence with Edward Said, Michel Foucault, Jacques Derrida and others. Like these thinkers, Hall was interested in shifting the grounds on which thought occurs and he aimed to change how we think by providing the tools and concepts needed to think critically. Thinking is not only for intellectuals, he believed; it is for everyone, and so enabling and equipping organic intellectuals was a lifelong project for Hall. Only if people could look beyond the surface of what appeared to be real, to their construction as symbolic systems signifying this or that, could they intervene in reconstructing reality.

Hall, for instance, saw nation-states as more than just political formations. He viewed them as systems of representation, symbolic entities that incorporated their subjects or citizens into homogeneous-seeming national cultures by subsuming difference and diversity. At the individual level a person's identity was in continuous formation, a negotiation between their "roots", or the cultures they were born into, and crucially the "routes" they travelled in the course of a lifetime.

What were Hall's roots and what were the routes that brought him to this place of global renown?

Hall was born in 1932 to a brown Jamaican family, a century after the abolition of slavery, when Jamaican society was still staggering to its feet from a history of enslavement and colonial subjugation.

In the pigmentocracies that ensued after emancipation from slavery, those who were phenotypically closer to the Caucasian ideal enjoyed a higher social rank than those closer to the other end of the spectrum. In his book *Black Skin, White Masks*, Frantz Fanon chronicles many of the psychological effects suffered by those disadvantaged by this system. Even one drop of white blood in the ancestral pool was valued more highly than any quantity of black blood, resulting in European heritage being more prized than African.

His parents, Herman and Jessie Hall, who married in 1918, were both mixed-race. Herman's mother was of Portuguese and Sephardic Jewish extraction, while Jessie Hopwood came from a well-established Port Antonio family endowed with fair complexion and social capital if not actual wealth. In those days, as it still is today in Jamaica, light skin was highly prized and Jessie was proud of hers, inherited from the white forebears sprinkled through her family tree.

In contrast, Herman Hall's lower-middle-class family, from rural Jamaica, was not as favourably equipped either with fair skin or social standing. But what Herman lacked in birthright he made up for with his industry and determination, rising to become the first non-white person to ascend the managerial ranks of the United Fruit Company.[2]

Both families were members of Jamaica's small middle class, although Jessie's was considered superior in social rank to Herman's. Equivalent to the "coloured" class in South Africa, brown Jamaicans were groomed to inherit the seats of power vacated by the former colonial masters. Years later, when discussing his childhood, Hall would say, "People think of Jamaica as a simple society. In fact, it had the most complicated color stratification system in the world. Talk about practical semioticians; anybody in my family could compute and calculate anybody's social status by grading the particular quality of their hair versus the particular quality of the family they came from and which street they lived in, induding physiognomy, shading, etc. You could trade off one characteristic against another. Compared with that, the normal class stratification system is absolute child's play" (*Essential Essays*, 2:74).

His mother, Jessie, was born to a teacher in the agricultural school in Port Antonio and the postmistress of the town, who was an "expert in racial classification", according to Hall (*Familiar Stranger*, 16). The family had breeding and colour (he suspected his mother's grandparents were white, judging by the colour of her mother, his maternal grandmother) but they were not particularly well-off and Jessie was soon adopted and raised by a wealthy aunt and uncle. She was schooled at Hampton, an exclusive Jamaican girls' school, considered England her home country and lived in the parish of Portland on a small property named Norwich, overlooking the sea, in a beautiful house that was later bought by the American singer Eartha Kitt.

Having grown up in such a prestigious family, Jessie feigned the spirit and attitudes of the small planter class. Her sister, Inez, whom Hall recalled living with their family for a while, was a study in contrast. Inez (or Hoppy, as she was known) had not benefited from affluent adopted parents and she was more down to earth, somewhat masculine, and much less obsessed with grooming and social striving.

Perhaps because she did not actually belong to the bourgeoisie by birth, Jessie became obsessed with maintaining the privileges acquired through adoption and saw to it that her husband and children adhered to the rarefied rituals and protocols that befitted an upper-class Jamaican family aspiring to whiteness. Young Hall rebelled against this, escaping whenever he could to the home of his paternal grandmother, Mammy Hall, in Old Harbour, on Jamaica's south coast.

A mischievous, musically inclined child, Hall felt at home in this lively place that was a hub of activity with relatives and friends popping in and out all day. His five maiden aunts doted on him and his cousin Maureen Clare, who later became a nun, rising to be the formidable principal of Immaculate Conception Girls' Convent School, housed at the former Constant Spring Hotel in Kingston.[3] Sister Maureen Clare remembers him as fun-loving and full of games and tricks. He was particularly fond of word games and playing jazz on the piano.

His lifelong passion for jazz began in his teens while listening to his older brother, George, play his jazz records. Hall learned to play the piano beautifully and aspired to be a musician, although he never had a formal music lesson in his life. Along with George, who was twelve years older, he had a sister, Patricia, five years older than him. The difference in their ages meant that Hall, being the youngest, was often left to his own devices.

His paternal family home in Old Harbour became a haven for the young boy. His vivacious maiden aunts were full of stories and banter and the kitchen overflowed with good food and drink. Hall found unconditional love and affection there, and it was also a gateway to a more varied and exciting Jamaica than the stifling world of his immediate family. His aunt Gerry had started a two-room school for neighbourhood children, preparing them for secondary school, when she was nineteen, and was still teaching spelling to a few when she reached the age of one hundred.[4] Next door to his grandmother's home was a Pentecostal church from which loud singing and clapping could be heard, and Hall relished his physical closeness to a black culture forbidden to his siblings and himself.

When Jessie visited her mother-in-law's home, it was as if she was a member of the upper class visiting her poor, provincial relatives in the countryside. Hall had little sympathy for her world view or her social pretensions, and grew up feeling more and more alienated from his mother and her obsession with British culture and the maintaining of colour boundaries. Her attitude of entitlement towards the staff whose labour she took for granted and her colonial outlook struck the young boy as being out of step with what was needed in a society looking forward to independence from Britain.

Hall's father, Herman, was an accountant at the United Fruit Company, a mild-mannered, quiet man who smoked cigars and sipped a rum and ginger in the evenings after work. Over the course of his career, Herman had risen from a lowly job in the financial department to become chief accountant at the firm, but it was his wife, Jessie, who ruled the roost. An ambitious and capable woman who might have thrived in public life had she had a job, Jessie focused her formidable talents on her family, making it, as Hall would say later, her career.[5]

Merton, their house in Kingston at Trevennion Park Road, a thriving middle-class neighbourhood off the central artery of Half Way Tree, was the arena in which she staged her incremental sorties towards full island royalty status. A retinue of servants waited on the family and their upwardly mobile friends and colleagues, supporting the estate-style life to which Jessie aspired. A tennis court was carefully created and maintained and formal tennis parties held, with the men dressed in long white pants and the women in tennis dresses. Despite being captain of his school team, Hall was only allowed to be a ball boy on home ground.

Appearances to the contrary, Herman's salary could barely accommodate the lifestyle Jessie had determined they deserved, leading to incessant quarrels about money and the lack of it. Hall viewed his family's pretensions with faint revulsion and longed to get away from it all.

On Sundays, Jessie would hold rum-punch gatherings at Merton and the Halls and their guests would engage in "verandah talk", during which they regaled each other with stories about everything from politics to world affairs to local gossip and bedroom scandals. None of them were church-goers or overly religious so Sunday was a day of leisure. Great care was exercised over whom the children could invite to their home. Only those of similar or higher social status could be invited. This meant that the only black people in the house were necessarily members of the service staff, who were confined to the nether regions of the house and its unmanicured backyard.

This backyard attracted young Hall much more than the meticulously constructed but emotionally barren social world of the main house. He gravitated towards the cook, Ethel, and the gardener, Cecil, who both came from the elusive other Jamaica that he yearned to know. He found out that Cecil was a leading figure in a native Baptist Revivalist sect that conducted mass baptisms in the Hope River on a Sunday, while Ethel and her friends would stop, after getting off work late at night, at Pentecostal yards in downtown Kingston for the evening service.

Hall was the only member of his immediate family to show an interest in church and religion even though he had no serious religious convictions. But he had been baptized in the Anglican church and enjoyed singing hymns; girls had surfaced on his adolescent horizon and one place to mingle with them was at church. For a couple of years, he joined Christian Endeavour, an American evangelical group that organized bus trips to towns and villages outside Kingston, where Revivalist meetings were held and the visitors would participate.

Sometimes the visitors were asked to lead the service and Hall, among others, was invited to preach. He took the opportunity to exercise his young social conscience, addressing the poverty and inequality surrounding him, and asking if this could indeed be what God had in mind when he was designing such a social system. These religious excursions allowed him to make the acquaintance of a wider range of people than he was accustomed to meeting at home. But his fascination with religion was not motivated merely by self-interest, as he would show much later with his study on Rastafari and other native Jamaican religions. It had been a central part of his childhood, and would remain of interest as a cultural institution. Hall would later realize that the Revival services he heard when he visited his grandmother, Mammy Hall, were Protestantism in the process of being creolized:

> Next to where my grandmother lived in Old Harbour, this very small country town, there was a revivalist church. My grandmother always marched the entire family out to the Anglican church, for Sunday worship. My aunt who had converted to Catholicism marched those who were left to the Catholic Church. Then the Catholic pastor and the Anglican priest came back for Sunday lunch. My father arrived from Kingston with all of us, you know, a huge country lunch. This is a tiny, tiny, poor house in Old Harbour, the most dusty part of Jamaica, and with my wonderful grandmother, who I adored, presiding over this. They would start to eat and drink; my father brought rum punch etc. While we were eating, across the road, the revivalist church began, first of all singing Moody and Sankey hymns. But gradually as the ceremonies over there progressed, the rhythm grew slower, it became more grounded, the bass began to come through and eventually it was a kind of African music. (*Personally Speaking*, 2).

Hall's early years saw Jamaica and the wider British West Indies, as the region was then known, going through a turbulent period. The year 1938, when he turned six, was a significant one in West Indian political history. Labour disturbances throughout the islands beginning in 1935 and culminating in 1937–38 with riots in Trinidad, Jamaica and Barbados led to the appointment of the Moyne Commission – a Royal Commission of Enquiry dispatched by the Colonial Office in the wake of the disturbances. On the basis of the investigations and recommendations of the commission, in 1944 Jamaica became self-governing – "under Crown super-vison". The new constitution, based on universal adult suffrage, granted Jamaicans greater control over their affairs.

Although Hall was only six in 1938, he was conscious of the import of the social upheaval from the effect it had on his own family. His mother, like many other upwardly mobile Anglophile elites, was dismayed by what the unrest implied for the balance of power in Jamaica. Despite the discomfort of his immediate family, these first stirrings of a population eager for independence and fed up with their lot in the twilight of the colonial era made a huge impact on young Hall's imagination.

In global terms these were also the war years. There was widespread turbulence in the world and the *Daily Gleaner* (Jamaica's main newspaper) was full of news about it, as almost nothing that happened locally was considered newsworthy enough to make the front page. The main pages of the *Gleaner* routinely reported a pot pourri of events from elsewhere.

The big bogey of the twentieth century was communism, which had established itself on the heels of World War I. The seeds of the infamous mid-century Cold War were sown by the Russian Revolution of 1917 when the peasants and working-class people revolted against the government of Tsar Nicholas II. This brought in the first communist government in the world, spawning a global movement designed to liberate workers from exploitative capitalist practices and create more humane, worker-oriented societies.

Communism polarized the world, dividing it into two oppositional power blocks. It spread across Europe, creating what became known as the Eastern Bloc, unifying the countries of East Germany, the Soviet Union, Poland, Czechoslovakia and Hungary. The Eastern Bloc was ideologically and geopolitically opposed to the West, the so-called free world, the countries of Western Europe, North America and their affiliates. Communist countries were organized around economic and social rights – among them the right to shelter, food and clothing – while capitalist countries claimed more of an interest in political rights and personal "freedom". Britain, France and the United States all established their societies on notions of liberty, equality and freedom, but the liberty and equality were only for some and no contradiction was seen between white liberty and the colonization of many other peoples. Perhaps their involvement in suppressing the freedom of millions in their colonies and slaveholdings gave Western countries special insight into the importance of liberty – thus free speech, free press, freedom to protest and freedom of association were considered more fundamental in the "free world".

Jamaica found itself aligned with the capitalist world by virtue of having been a colony of one of the most well-established empires in the West, Britain. In colonial countries across the world, communist parties sprouted, in response to the widely circulated writings of German political philosophers Karl Marx and Friedrich Engels. *The Communist Manifesto*, originally published in 1848, went viral, as the working classes of the world and those who argued on their behalf found representation in its stirring call to unite.

At his high school in Kingston, Jamaica College, Hall, like many other youngsters around the world, was exposed to Marx's manifesto and accompanying literature. The arguments had a resonance, particularly in societies still under colonial rule where the labouring classes were treated with little respect. The need for social justice in the newly burgeoning society was overwhelming and reading Marx, Lenin and other communist writers, with their call for better wages and working conditions, struck the young Hall forcefully, making him a socialist for life.

The United Fruit Company, where his father worked, was an early example of the exploitative multinational companies that spread across the region and the world, giving rise to the term neocolonialism. Their practices were extractive, relying on cheap labour with little concern for working conditions or the well-being of the countries in which they operated.

To understand the family and class Hall was born into, it is important to go back a century or more. The new society of Jamaica emerged after the passing of the Act for the Abolition of Slavery in 1833, but abolition of plantation slavery was anything but straightforward. The act stipulated that children under six were to be freed immediately. Everyone else was to undergo a six-year period of apprenticeship to groom the formerly enslaved for wage labour. The apprenticeship system turned out to be a failure for various reasons, chief among them the fact that the planters still existed and had difficulty adjusting to their loss of absolute power. The formerly enslaved, having been liberated of the compulsion to provide labour, could not understand why they should work for anyone else now that they were free. In this sense, the act defeated its main purpose, which was the creation of an efficient society of free people.

The economy made its official transition to a free economy in 1834. While the planters were generously compensated by the British government for the loss of their enslaved people, no effort was made to encourage the growth of an independent peasantry, as planters saw this as a potential threat to their estates. As a result, planters refused to sell land to individuals in small lots and it was only when missionary organizations intervened, buying land in bulk and selling or leasing it to small farmers, that a post-emancipation economy began to develop.

Some formerly enslaved became squatters, cultivating an existence in inaccessible hilly areas and contributing to the slow but steady growth of a peasant economy. Those unable to leave the estates remained and became wage labourers – the basis for the landless working class or "proletariat" of today. Jamaican society lurched along for a while, with a narrow European ruling class in charge, the planters still trying to oppose every attempt to create a more just and free society. At the same time, sugar, the single crop they produced, was facing competition from other parts of the world. These problems were compounded by the introduction of indentured workers from India and China to provide cheap labour on the plantations after the failure of apprenticeship.

Social strife became widespread, with what was known as the Jamaica Rebellion, better known today as the Morant Bay

Rebellion, taking place in 1865. This unbalanced state of affairs only began to change after the introduction of banana cultivation by American businesses in 1867. Bananas required less tending and were therefore amenable to peasant cultivation. It was also a peasant crop that could be exported, so bananas became the foundation for a more viable economy.

Much later in life Hall was mortified to realize that on his mother's side, the family had once been slaveholders. One relative by marriage, John Rock Grosset, had been a prominent anti-abolitionist and pro-slavery pamphleteer.[6] No wonder his own mother, Jessie, pined after a plantation-style life, what Hall thought of as the "colonial family romance" he was determined to escape. Jessie insisted, for instance, that her family name, Hopwood, was the English version of "Habsburg", hinting at connections to the Austrian royal family. His mother's world view was a "structure of feeling", a common set of perceptions and values shared by her generation, that Hall found suffocating and intolerable, especially as it played out in his immediate family.

"For such individuals there is a conscious ideal of identification with the European or Englishman," wrote anthropologist Fernando Henriques in his study *Family and Colour in Jamaica*. Except for the gender identification in the following quote, Henriques could have been talking about Hall's imperious mother when he said "the coloured person" in the West Indies represented a "unique phenomenon": "He is generally almost entirely ignorant of African culture and despises what little he does know as being primitive and concerned with the undesirable, that is, the black. According to his colour he is prey to much anxiety as to whether he will be able to achieve or has achieved acceptance by the white minority. Even if this ideal is unattainable there is still the conscious anxiety to appear white in his ways and ideas."[7]

School provided an escape valve for Hall. Jamaica College was a tropical Eton, its beautiful colonial-style campus nestled in the "lawns of Liguanea" with the magnificent Blue Mountain range as backdrop. As one of his schoolfriends, Charles Levy, would later write: "The world of Jamaica College was, like Caesar's Gaul, divided into three parts: There were 'Old Boys', former students who had achieved Nirvana; there were 'present boys' who enjoyed the legacy left behind by their predecessors; and then there were 'new boys'."[8] "New boys" were subjected to ragging by "present boys" from which they could escape only by answering the question "Do you have a sister?" in the affirmative. As Hall had a sister, he was able to offer her name to his seniors and avert the worst of the ragging.

Facing Jamaica College at the time, on what is now Old Hope Road, were orchards of Bombay mangoes, converted now into a housing development called Mona. It was a ritual for new boys to participate in at least one raid on the orchards, which were patrolled by rangers on horseback. Legend had it that two boys were once caught by a ranger with stolen fruit and taken to the Matilda's Corner police station, from where headmaster Reginald Murray later secured their release. It was reported that after caning them, Murray asked the boys if they knew why they had been punished; when they answered that it was for stealing mangoes, the headmaster corrected them, saying no, it was for being *caught* stealing mangoes.

Kingston today is unrecognizable from Kingston of the 1940s, but Jamaica College is one of the few places remaining that looks exactly as it did all those years ago. Its environs, however, are completely changed. In those days, trams ran from Half Way Tree, carrying passengers to Hope Gardens past Jamaica College to the terminus in Papine, and another rite of passage for new boys was to "hop the tram", stylishly jumping on it while it was still moving and alighting before it came to a complete stop.

Hall, known as "S.M." at school, is remembered as a quick-witted, sharp-voiced youngster who loved to play games, going on to become head of the tennis team, the cadet corps and eventually head boy of Jamaica College. There were early signs of what are now referred to as "leadership qualities". A schoolmate described an occasion when a group of six or seven students who took the bus from Cross Roads to school in the mornings "were having to encounter the rough manner of workmen travelling to Papine to work on the university hospital building. Stuart one morning assembled us and directed 260-pounder Trevor 'Flebby' Hylton to take the lead, 'Long John' – that was me – to follow behind and the others to line up in descending order of height. On his command to 'charge' we torpedoed our way towards the bus door."[9]

High schools such as Jamaica College were incubators for political, business and social elites who would one day take over from the British. The curriculum was designed to inculcate students into British ways of thinking and living and consisted almost exclusively of traditional subjects taught to English schoolchildren. There was almost no local content, and Hall would often wonder, "To learn what they knew, did one have to become like them?" (*Familiar Stranger*, 118).

There was only one booklet published by the local newspaper, the *Daily Gleaner*, which introduced students briefly to the geography and history of Jamaica while skirting the traumatic history of enslavement and enforced servitude upon which the country was built. When Hall was fourteen, the Institute of Jamaica opened a library with a special section for young adults. He practically lived there after that. By the time he reached sixth form, a current affairs/modern history course had been added to the Cambridge Higher Schools curriculum and the young Jamaican lapped up the more contemporary historical focus it afforded. Reading about the rise of fascism, the causes of World War II, Lenin and the Russian Revolution, the "scourge" of communism and the origins of the Cold War stimulated young Hall, who followed current events in *Keesing's Contemporary Archives*, a weekly newspaper available along with British Council pamphlets on the iniquities of the Russian Revolution and Lenin.

All of this brought history alive for Hall and his schoolmates, although no connections were made to slavery, emancipation or the growing demand for universal suffrage. He became obsessed with the theatre of war which dominated his years at Jamaica College. He played war games tracking the incursions, invasions, attacks of European countries avidly, fascinatedly following the invasion of the Far East, learning about Asia from the US occupation of the Philippines, for example, and in the process educating himself on geopolitics and history.

If World War II dominated Hall's global horizon, his mother dominated the domestic one, ruling over her family like a petty autarch. Jessie's totalitarian regime demanded complete capitulation from her husband and children, for whom she had little regard once they submitted to her authority. He was the only one who successfully resisted her, although eventually he had to make his escape to remain independent. The trouble started when he grew old enough to have his own interests and positions on things, arousing his mother's antagonism:

> She wanted to dominate me, but she also despised those whom she dominated. So she despised my father because he would give in to her. She despised my sister, because she was a girl, and as my mother said, women were not interesting. In adolescence, my sister fought her all along, but once my mother broke her, she despised her. So we had that relationship of antagonism. I was the youngest. She thought I was destined to oppose her but she respected me for that. Eventually when she knew what I had become in England – fulfilling all her most paranoid fantasies of the rebellious son – she didn't want me to come back to Jamaica, because by then I would've represented my own thing, rather than her image of me. She found out about my politics and said, "Stay over there, don't come back here and make trouble for us with those funny ideas."[10]

By the 1940s, life in Jamaica was beginning to succumb to the influence of American culture, which arrived via Hollywood movies and jazz. Every Saturday, Hall and his friends went to the cinema, after which they made up games based on the cowboy films, romance stories or war thrillers they had just seen. He was particularly fond of goose-stepping like an SS officer, complete with monocle and boots. There were dance parties with the latest American dances and tentative sexual exploration in their aftermath.

At home, however, it was as if everyone had been immaculately conceived. Sex was a taboo subject and Hall felt confused and misguided by the juvenile chatter of school friends about what exactly it entailed. His brother was so much older than him, and had deteriorating eyesight that did not encourage an active social life; little enlightenment was forthcoming from that quarter. George was considered the clever one and wrote short stories and poetry, though he had studied agricultural chemistry in the United States, returning to work at Caymanas sugar estate until he went blind.

Patricia, his older sister, was more outgoing and sociable, fraternizing and talking about the opposite sex with her friends. She was a vibrant, feisty young woman who unfortunately soon fell victim to their mother's fantasies of high birth and her dedication to upkeep of the family's light complexion, leaving both siblings scarred for life. The tragedy was not an uncommon one. Young Pat fell in love with a medical student from Barbados who had come to study at the newly founded University College of the West Indies. Although his social status was on par with theirs, even surpassing that of the Halls in later life, his black skin meant he was considered unsuitable by Jessie Hall as a husband for her daughter. She had no qualms about putting an end to the budding romance.

After the forcible break-up of her relationship with the medical student, Pat suffered a breakdown. She was then subjected to psychiatric treatment, including electroconvulsive therapy, which reduced her to a listless state from which she never quite recovered. Trained as a personal secretary, Pat never worked again but devoted herself to looking after the family, and her older brother George, who was already going blind.

Pat's breakdown affected Hall profoundly, making him flirt with the idea of becoming a psychoanalyst, driven by the desire to help his sister. It was Pat's predicament that made Hall realize that Jamaica's deeply ingrained racism and classism were not merely playing out in the unconscious of the individuals involved but were "a kind of cultural configuration we were living out as a colonial culture" (*Personally Speaking*, 6). His family was living out a colonial fantasy that would devour him as well, if allowed.

Hall had already undergone an emotional separation from his family, estranged, as he felt, from their carefully constructed cocoon of class privilege. Depressed, he gradually withdrew from them, telling them as little as possible about his activities, and gravitating more and more towards the political consciousness he found developing among the older students at Jamaica College. The thought of a more inclusive, less hierarchical and racially divided society beginning to seem possible in pre-independence Jamaica was seductive and young Hall grasped after it eagerly. While on the one hand it seemed he was acting out a phase of teenage rebellion, taking off on his bicycle for extended periods of time without telling anyone where he was going, he was also embodying the tensions and psychic costs of growing up in the midst of intense social transformation.

Americanization in Jamaica was not by any means confined to popular culture and ice-cream parlours. In the late war years, the Left Book Club was formed in Kingston and a meeting held at the Readers and Writers Club where the activist and journalist W.A. Domingo gave a talk on the youth movement in the United States. Domingo described American youth as disillusioned by the heritage of the post-war years and "determined to make a new social order by their cooperative effort". An editor of *Garvey's World* who had been part of the Harlem Renaissance, Domingo suggested that "their example could well be patterned by their confreres in Jamaica" ("Club Notes", *Daily Gleaner*, 17 January 1939). At the same club, one H.P. Jacobs was preparing to give a talk titled "Modern Capitalism and the Various Symptoms Which Such a System Is Bound to Display". He had previously given a talk on economic theory.

It is clear that in the 1930s and 1940s, Jamaica was far from a colonial backwater out of touch with the rest of the world. At least there seems to have been a thirst for knowledge and new ideas. When British Council adviser Sir Harold Standard visited Jamaica in 1943 and talked of the interest in Britain in adult education, he could scarcely have imagined that one of the brightest lights of adult education in Britain in the latter half of the twentieth century, the Open University's Professor Stuart Hall, was right then at school in Kingston.

Hall's nighttime lectures on BBC2 would make him a

household name and face in 1980s Britain, but in the 1940s at Jamaica College, he was spending more and more time in the library poring over left-wing publications. There he also discovered Freud's theories of psychoanalysis and briefly flirted with the notion of medical school and training to become a psychoanalyst. He applied his newly gleaned knowledge to analysing his sister's illness, recognizing that her breakdown was a literal expression of not just the personal tragedy she had experienced, but the trauma of the end days of colonialism and the procrustean demands of the colonial family. It was then he realized that his only chance of escape from a similar fate was to win a scholarship and leave the island.

TWO

fter finishing at Jamaica College in 1950, where he excelled in both sporting and academic endeavours, Hall proceeded to Knox College in the interior of Jamaica to attend its summer Adult Education Institute. He had done well at school and a photo in the *Daily Gleaner* of 8 July 1950 shows him in school uniform with a caption saying, "S.M. Hall, Head Boy of Jamaica College, is seen receiving one of the many prizes he won at the annual prize-giving function held at the College Wednesday, from His Lordship Bishop Dale."

Before that, on 16 May 1950 the *Daily Gleaner* reported that, at age eighteen, Stuart Hall, "son of Mr. H.M. Hall, Division Accountant of the United Fruit Company", had won the "additional" Jamaica Scholarship awarded that year. He was head boy of Jamaica College and tennis captain at the time. The Jamaica Scholarship is a prestigious award given once a year to the best student in the island. That year, exceptionally, two were awarded. Hall had passed his Cambridge Higher School Certificate with flying colours the year before but was too young to qualify for a scholarship then. Taking no chances, he also applied for the Rhodes Scholarship in 1950, proceeding to summer school at Knox College in Spaldings in the interim.

The programme for the summer school succinctly proclaimed its orientation. "In keeping with the widespread and growing interest in Adult Community Education in Jamaica, the 1950 Knox College Summer School will be concerned with 'Education for Adults'." In the mornings students attended a course of lectures on the subject of adult education given by Margaret Read, head of the Colonial Department of the University of London's Institute of Education. Practical workshops were conducted in such weighty topics as "The Use and Care of the Land", "The Use and Care of Money", "Education for Citizenship", "Adult Education through the Labour Movement", and "Sex and Family Education".

After tea there were creative activity groups in music, art, drama, writing and other aesthetic endeavours. The well-known painter Albert Huie and sculptor Edna Manley were some of those involved in the art classes, and the list of workshop instructors and lecturers read like a who's who of prominent Jamaican educators, social activists and other luminaries, among them D.T.M. Girvan, Philip Sherlock, Robert Verity and Gloria Cumper.

Hall stayed on and worked at Knox College after the summer school ended, finding life in Spaldings, a distance away from his family in Kingston, refreshing. On 17 October 1950, he received a telegram that said, "Please attend Kings House Friday 20th at 4.30 pm for interview reference Rhodes

Scholarship entry." The next day he sent a telegram to his family saying, "Received Rhodes telegram coming for Friday interview."

Detailed advice on how to conduct himself during the interview arrived in a letter from his sister, Pat: "Trust Mr. Manley will not pose any brain twisters. Don't be in too much of a hurry to rush into your answers. That impressive pause – three seconds – . . . can cover a multitude of sins and is apt to prevent one using plural verbs with singular subjects. . . . I expect that you will address the company at large as 'Gentlemen', and individuals either by name or as 'Sir' which shows an attitude of respect without servility." Tongue-in-cheek, Pat continued, "You will take three deep breaths as you are entering the room and you will not flirt with McGillivray's daughters – if any – while you wait your turn."

The decision of the interview committee must have been swift, for by 21 October, Hall and his family were already getting telegrams congratulating them on his being named the Jamaica Rhodes Scholar for 1951 and for winning both of the most prestigious scholarships the island had to offer. After surrendering the now redundant Jamaica Scholarship, Hall was admitted to Merton College at Oxford, something his delighted mother took as a sign of manifest destiny, since the name of their family home in Trevennion Park, Kingston, was Merton.

He was equally delighted, and practised writing his name on the back of one of his exam envelopes in cursive style: *Mr Stuart Hall. Mr Stuart M. Hall.* At the age of nineteen, he was finally on his way, leaving Jamaica for Oxford, England, where he would do a bachelor's degree in English literature. "All you do, do not come back with any half-baked ideas on the equal rights of man," wrote one friend, bidding him farewell.

For Jessie Hall, her son being awarded the Rhodes was a dream come true. Neither she nor Herman had been to university and they dearly wished their younger son would fulfil their ambitions by studying in England. Their elder son had gone to university in the United States but now all Jessie's aspirations for bona fide Britishness were about to materialize via her talented younger son. Not only was he going to college in England, he was going to the best university the mother country could offer. With alacrity, Jessie proceeded to equip Hall for life at Oxford, complete with an enormous steamer trunk that her son, alas, abandoned as soon as he had settled into Merton College.

Mother and son set off on an Elders and Fyffes banana boat (a firm associated with the United Fruit Company, where his father worked) as second-class passengers. The Halls boarded the boat in Port Antonio, where it finally arrived after collecting bananas from different ports around the island. Within a few hours of leaving they encountered Hurricane Charlie, on its way to ravage Jamaica. The ship plunged in and out of the enormous waves the storm produced, thrilling young Hall, though the catastrophic weather must have terrified his mother.

Arriving in England in August, the Halls had weeks to kill before the Oxford term started in October. They spent their time sightseeing, visiting historic tourist spots such as Westminster Abbey, the Houses of Parliament and Buckingham

Palace. Hall and his mother stayed at Methodist International House, a haven for foreign students in London run by a church. The atmosphere in the hostel was religious, with an attached chapel and grace at meals and hymn singing, but with its international outlook, it afforded him a less rigidly English introduction to London. Here he met students from African and Asian countries as well as the Caribbean. One of the first people he met was A.N.R. Robinson, the future prime minister and president of Trinidad and Tobago.

Hall was well schooled in the ways of the mother country. He was nothing if not a "colonial". He had been taught to admire the British way of life, its culture and imagination through the novels he studied, the history he read and the political institutions to which he and his fellow students had been exposed. Young, brown, middle-class Jamaicans like himself were groomed to take over the reins of governance once the British left. Yet he was nagged by the persistent suspicion that he could never be authentically British or possessed of colonial values, ideals and conventions by birthright.

The enigma of Hall's arrival in England was compounded by his delighted discovery of the same "black folk" he thought he had left back home now in London, where they had come looking for better opportunities than Jamaica presented. Arriving by ship, the new migrants huddled together, their clothing barely protecting them from the harsh cold of England. Though he and they came from different rungs of the social ladder, they were all the outside children of empire, tolerated but not by any means welcome.

It was this surreal encounter in faraway England that laid the foundation for Hall's later preoccupation with diaspora as a hermeneutic device. Finding himself a member of the Caribbean/Jamaican diaspora, along with the Jamaican migrants who arrived in England from 1948 onwards, he would later marshal the "diasporic experience" as a productive interpretive tool for explaining the complex inner relations of this late phase of colonialism and the contemporary postcolonial moment.

In the meantime, Merton College beckoned. Hall and his mother went to visit the rooms he would occupy there, carrying his enormous trunk. The trunk proved too heavy to carry up to the first floor, where his room was, and remained consigned to the basement. After bringing up some of his clothes and personal effects from the basement, he forgot about the trunk, regarding it literally as unwelcome baggage from the life he had left behind.

Today, Hall is one of a dozen "eminent Mertonians" listed on the website of the college along with Sir Thomas Bodley, T.S. Eliot, J.R.R. Tolkien and Theodor Adorno. Since 2017 the college has offered a doctoral-level scholarship in his name to deserving scholars, enabling new generations of creative thinkers to challenge the status quo and provoke original thinking, debate and research, while illuminating connections between politics, culture and society.

When Hall arrived in Oxford from Jamaica in 1951, he would scarcely have imagined such an eventuality. Merton College, founded in 1264, with its classic Oxford architecture, struck him as a place of "medieval seriousness, solidity and gloom" (*Familiar Stranger*, 155). He was shocked to find that the library had sections where the books were chained to the shelves to prevent theft. His coursework included texts in Anglo-Saxon, Middle English, High German and Old Norse, impossibly foreign languages to the young Jamaican, who felt plunged into the remote, icy depths of Englishness.

College life consisted of bland meals in hall that Hall doubted he could stomach for too long. The war having ended not so long before, rationing was still in force and students were allotted ration books which had to be turned in at the start of the term. His two-room quarters were heated by a gas fire, on which he would warm crumpets to have with his tea.

The college environs were beautifully manicured, with sweeping views of Christ Church Meadow. But the communal baths were a distance away from his quarters, a cold walk through freezing weather to reach cavernous, white-tiled baths. The young men went in groups, carrying books to read while waiting their turn to bathe.

Hall was usually the solitary non-white in these groups and often felt intensely self-conscious, although he tried not to betray this. In Jamaica he would have been considered "brown" rather than "black", a major ethnic and class difference, but in England such fine distinctions were lost. The few black students were treated politely, viewed as quaint rather than threatening presences. "When are you going home?" was a question they frequently faced, though it was not meant to be hostile. As an undergraduate he encountered little overt racism but was intensely conscious of his difference in terms of race and colour. As it turned out, he was the only black student at Merton, though there were a few South Asian students there as well.

Together with several others at Oxford, Hall found himself part of a deeply committed West Indian group – the West Indian Society – looking forward to the coming of independence and impending self-government in their respective islands. He made friends with the Trinidadian students, who constituted the largest West Indian group, many of whom were older – bright civil servants sent by their government for higher studies in areas like development economics. V.S. Naipaul, the famous writer from Trinidad, was also at Oxford studying literature at the same time as Hall. Naipal was at University College, one of a small number of West Indian undergraduates at university there. Hall did not warm to Naipaul, who never went to West Indian Society meetings or mingled with West Indians, especially black ones. (Hall once heard Naipaul refer to the great C.L.R. James as "that vain black old man" in a public lecture at the South Bank.)

The West Indian Society included men like J. O'Neil Lewis and Doddridge Alleyne, with whom Hall played squash. Alleyne later became the most senior and trusted civil servant in the government of Eric Williams, the first prime minister of independent Trinidad and Tobago. There were others like William Demas, who was at Cambridge, and Max Ifill. Another Trinidadian at Cambridge was the formidable Lloyd Best, who later became one of Williams's most vociferous critics and opponents. Best later acknowledged Hall as a great influence. Thus Hall found himself in the midst of a number of students who would go on to become stalwarts of the independence generation in the postcolonial Caribbean.

In his posthumously published memoir, Hall recalled the vigorous, stimulating debates the group engaged in on the impending independence and future of the Caribbean, which they imagined as an integrated political entity, a federation of West Indian islands. They looked forward eagerly to the roles they would play when their respective countries became independent, and to enacting the rapid decolonization of the region.

As they were Caribbean people, their solemn preoccupations were enlivened by the high-spirited, lively character for which the region was known. Hall particularly recalled a Trinidadian student named Noel Henwood, who said he was both a member of the Communist Party and a priest in an African sect.

It was in this milieu that Hall began to practise his burgeoning diasporic West Indian identity, becoming West Indian rather than Jamaican. He was very much part of the Caribbean Artists' Movement and generally spent a lot of time at the West Indian Students' Centre hanging out with the "bearded radicals" his parents had warned him against.

Henwood was president of the Oxford University West Indian Society. In 1954 Hall and Henwood, along with a few others, attempted to start a publication titled *Caribbean Journal* to address their concerns and aspirations as young West Indians. Hall's commitment to lifelong education – adult education – nurtured at Knox College in Jamaica, duly manifested itself.

"This is a publication from students to students," read the first draft editorial:

> We are using the word "student" with its widest connotation. We mean all those who are seriously engaged, whether in a formal way or not, with the problems that face us at the present time. It is not too much to say that, from the broadest point of view, the task facing the West Indies at the moment is a task of education: the "drawing forth" of the creative sources of life in every field, in order that we may create for ourselves a world in which, for the first time, we can find identity, meaning and security. Education does not end when the days of school and university are over and if it is to be meaningful, must continue as long as life itself.[11]

The commitment to lifelong learning and ideas is already in evidence and the idea of forming a "nation" out of the individual island states is also articulated:

> We are committed to the belief that there is something to be gained by the generation of ideas and discussion, the free play and exchange of views by people who are drawn together by a community of interests. We are committed to the belief that this is a historic moment in the evolution of our national culture, and that we – all of us – are the people who must speak, lest we find ourselves in the not-too-distant future committed to a world we did not make or desire.

The growth of a West Indian consciousness and identity is manifest in the first proposed editorial:

> The fact that this attempt to reach West Indians wherever they may be comes from Oxford, is, to our minds, of far less importance than the fact that it has originated from a group of

people who have been forced by circumstance to conceive of themselves as West Indian; who have been forced to face the consequences of this discovery; who have been made to feel how vitally creative this sense of identity can be; and who have grown to see this fact as their only hope of salvation. It is this, more than anything else, which we are trying in some way both to express and evoke. Our hope is to infect anyone and everyone with this sense of identity, with a sense of commitment in a struggle from which none are free to exclude themselves, and, above all, with a sense of the urgency of the times: to see a way in which we all, by realistic action, may realize our common aims and aspirations in some form of meaningful, creative achievement.

The young and feisty students debated independence and self-government with visiting Caribbean intellectuals and the writers already in London, such as Edgar Mittelholzer, George Lamming, Sam Selvon, Andrew Salkey and Jan Carew. This was the group that formed the first generation of Caribbean writers in the immediate pre-independence years. They were all mobilized into writing for the BBC's *Caribbean Voices* radio programme pioneered by Henry Swanzy. It was the support they received from Swanzy and the BBC that nurtured early West Indian literature. Hall was an aspiring poet and novelist in those days and also did some work with *Caribbean Voices*. His writings were published in magazines such as *Bim* and *Savacou*.

Hall also read the new Caribbean scholars who were emerging at the University College of the West Indies, founded in Kingston, Jamaica, in 1948. People such as Elsa Goveia, Edward Brathwaite (later Kamau), Douglas Hall, Roy

Augier, M.G. Smith and Arthur Lewis, who later won the
Nobel Prize in economics, had started examining and writing
about regional issues. Shockingly, it was only during this
period in London that he learned anything significant about
the other islands in the Caribbean. Because of Jamaica's
location in the north, closer to Cuba and Haiti, interaction
with the rest of the Caribbean had been minimal. In the
eastern and southern Caribbean in contrast, there was much
migration back and forth between the closely clustered
islands.

In the West Indian diaspora that developed in Britain,
migrants from different islands were forced to shed their
national identities and band together as West Indians. This
was what the editorial had referenced by saying that the
students had been "forced by circumstance to conceive of
themselves as West Indian". To begin with, it soon became
obvious that to the British they were all seen as having the
same racial/ethnic identity – often misidentified as Jamaican.
As they settled into their new homes and workplaces, the
creolization of British cities began in earnest, arousing the
resentment of the working-class British, who viewed the West
Indians as interlopers. This pushback further reinforced the
sense of a diasporic West Indian identity.

It was natural in such a climate for there to be great
sympathy for a federation of the relatively small islands of the
Caribbean into a larger, more powerful polity. This further
united the university students from the Caribbean, who felt
that collaborating against common adversaries would give the
West Indies a better chance of postcolonial prosperity. Today

the plans for a federated West Indies are hardly remembered but Norman Manley eloquently captured the situation facing the Caribbean at the first conference broaching the idea of federation. It was 1947 and the meeting was in Montego Bay:

> Here we all are on a sea of world conditions, stormy and hazardous in the extreme, each huddled in some little craft of our own. Some hardly have oars and only a few have accomplished a rudimentary sail to take them along. And here offered us is a boat, substantial, capable of being made sea-worthy and ready to be manned by our own captains and our own crew. If we don't leave our little boats and get into that larger vessel which is able to carry us to the goal of our ambitions, then I say without hesitation that we are damned and purblind and history will condemn us.[12]

In 1958 the ten territories of Antigua and Barbuda, Barbados, Dominica, Grenada, Jamaica, Montserrat, the then St Kitts-Nevis-Anguilla, St Lucia, St Vincent, and Trinidad and Tobago came together to form the West Indies Federation. The federal motto was "to dwell together in unity", but there was no agreement among the ten countries in the federation as to whether the power to regulate industrial development, freedom of movement and the collection of taxes should rest with the federal government or the individual island state governments. There was also disagreement about parliamentary representation for the member states.

The cracks in the federation grew wider and in 1961, the people of Jamaica voted in a referendum not to remain part of the regional entity. Basically, Jamaicans could not see what advantage there was in a coalition with a number of what they

considered small, insignificant islands and they were suspicious of being run by a government external to their territory
over which they would have little control. The federal
government did not survive the departure of Jamaica, with
the Trinidadian prime minister Eric Williams famously
saying, "One from ten leaves nought."

For Hall and the other West Indians, their political
allegiance was more to a federated government than to the
individual islands they came from. Yet island nationalism pre-
vailed in the end. The disappointment of the collapse of
federation affected Hall profoundly, colouring his political
outlook and blunting his regionalist tendencies. The impetus
to return to Jamaica became less urgent and he began paying
attention to local British political struggles, and the impact
these were having on West Indian migrants.

Hall also focused on finishing his degree in English
literature, drifting towards a group of American students at
Oxford, even though many of them were older than him,
having graduated from American universities with a first
degree already. Through the American scholars, with whom
young Hall discussed literature and criticism, he discovered
the work of American writers such as Herman Melville,
Henry Thoreau, Walt Whitman and also younger writers such
as Ernest Hemingway and F. Scott Fitzgerald.

After only one year at his college quarters, Hall moved with
some of the Americans into a north Oxford boarding house
whose other residents were older or retired Oxonians. The
Americans had more resources than Hall but they all
managed to have an active social life and enjoy themselves

though the Americans had an easier time adjusting to England than he did.

For his postgraduate degree, he was interested in examining the muckraking tradition of American realism, writers such as Sinclair Lewis, Upton Sinclair and Dos Passos. Unfortunately, the rigid Oxford curriculum did not recognize these authors as being worthy of study at the time so he decided on another American writer, Henry James, to whose novels he had been introduced by Walt Litz, an American scholar who had become his close friend and housemate.

Those were the years following the publication of *The Great Tradition* by F.R. Leavis, in 1948. In this hugely influential book, pre-eminent literary critic Leavis argued that James, despite being an American writer, belonged no less to the great tradition of English novelists than he did to the American canon, being by birth and upbringing from "the refined civilization of the old European America".[13] He was thus more comfortable in Europe than in the United States, the country of his birth, something that American literary critics censured him for.

With young Hall's Marxist leanings, Henry James seemed like a surprising choice to many, with his focus on the propertied middle classes, but what Hall had in common with James was their cultural difference from the English. In James's case, it was the intersection of the United States with England. "If from the English point of view he is unmistakably an American, he is also very much a European," said Leavis of James. Reading James, an American writer examining Englishness, and commenting on things English, at the very moment when he himself was encountering Englishness in that bastion of English civilization, Oxford, resonated deeply with Hall.

It was this "double consciousness" that Hall felt he had in common with the American writer. Straddling two worlds as he had done, at the juncture between a Jamaica to which he was not sure how to belong and England, to which he knew he did not belong, he connected deeply with the work of Henry James, much to the astonishment and disapproval of Marxist historian E.P. Thompson, who exclaimed, "How can you be interested in Henry James?" (*Familiar Stranger*, 217).

But Hall knew that what he appreciated about James was his extreme sensitivity to the nuances of English life, his grasp of the moral vacuum at the centre of wealth and sophistication, and how the refinement and exquisite taste of his middle- and upper-class characters coexisted with a crude and venal self-interest, "the corruption secreted at the heart of a refined class self-confident in its own ethical superiority" (*Familiar Stranger*, 217). He understood the complexity of cultural translation, the finely tuned distinctions between American and European versions of civilization. Years later, in his memoir, Hall would declare that he had no regrets about choosing to study James. Indeed, after his death in 2014, he was buried with a heavily annotated copy of James's *Portrait of a Lady*.

Much later also, Hall would acknowledge the importance of F.R. Leavis, calling him the most perceptive and influential literary critic in England, to the formation of cultural studies. Leavis's methodology involved the close reading of literary texts, but also of the culture they and their authors were embedded in. No one was more suited, Leavis believed, to grasping and assessing the broader culture of society than literary critics, and he urged them to take on the much wider historic task of interpreting and judging the trends and movements in the culture itself, in effect to undertake cultural criticism as well as literary criticism.

In the shift from literary theory to the cultural, however, Hall, like English critics Raymond Williams and Richard Hoggart before him, found himself at odds with Leavis, whose conception of culture was "the best that has been thought and said". This outlook excluded popular culture as culture worth reading and understanding on the grounds that it was not the product of refined minds, nor would it lead to the refinement of sensibilities.

Leavis viewed the role of the critic as that of a gatekeeper straining impurities and dross from the great tradition, to arrive at a select and choice group of literary works worth canonizing. "Only a lower-middle-class puritan could have entered into a tradition which was not his own and become its gatekeeper, its refiner, its gardener, the way Leavis did," remarked Hall in 1983 (*Cultural Studies*, 218).

Despite his divergence from the Leavis orthodoxy where popular culture was concerned, Hall acknowledged the critic's influence on his own views of literature as an essential component of a liberal education. Already at that early stage, just barely finished with his first degree, he was articulating views about the importance of dissolving the barriers between disciplines such as economics, sociology, psychology and political science – the social sciences – and the study of literature. "It is just possible that the future of human studies in universities . . . may come to depend to an increasing extent upon the degree to which the disciplines of literature and the social sciences are permitted to interact creatively," he wrote in a paper for the West Indian Society in 1956 titled "Notes for a New Science – 'Fiction and Income per Head': A Study of Reading Attitudes".

As an Oxford undergraduate, Hall was well on his way towards breaching disciplinary barriers while casting a sceptical eye at the shortcomings of studying human behaviour with the cold rationality of pure science. The study of literature and literary criticism, in his opinion, was the indispensable hermeneutic practice to assist in a rounded education. Not literature as the study of purely formal, stylistic expression but the study of literature along with the culture it was embedded in, and the context in which it was produced, as Leavis was proposing. "The function of literature is to bestow with moral and emotional meaning the apparent waste and futility of human experience," declared young Hall.

At Oxford, however, F.R. Leavis did not command anywhere near the same admiration and respect as Hall had for the literary critic. Ironically, considering his own elitist outlook, Leavis was considered "vulgar" and too serious by the Oxford literati, who had little regard for theory and criticism, literary or otherwise. Hall and his friends, on the other hand, avidly devoured each issue of *Scrutiny*, the critical journal founded by Leavis, along with other journals such as *Partisan Review* and the *Sewanee Review*.

This period of his life marked the culmination of Hall's disengagement from Oxford and its narrow, elitist ways. He was also increasingly becoming less interested in the study of novels and literature per se, drawn more and more to the study of culture and modernism and the puzzle of whether someone like him, coming from a backwater such as Jamaica, could ever be a "modern" subject. Could he ever confidently lay claim to modernist ideas and their ethos?

It was a puzzle. What was modernity? Could Caribbean people be modern? Or was it a condition reserved for Europeans and Americans? Was it an attitude of mind and a new way of being rather than a chronological period? The concept of the modern seemed to represent a rupture with tradition, a paradigmatic shift from old forms and styles toward a hitherto unattained stage of human development whose hallmark was newness and originality.

It seemed to Hall that modernity was part of a civilizational race in which colonized people like himself were at a considerable disadvantage (*Familiar Stranger*, 219). Was there only one pathway to modernity that excluded people from the periphery, and relegated them permanently to mimic it from a distance, always experiencing it second-hand? Had the idea of the modern itself been, like everything else, appropriated and colonized by the West?

Later Hall would agree with C.L.R. James's notion of the fundamentally modern nature of plantation society, arguing that plantation slavery as an institution was intimately linked to the development of modernness, creating the possibility of a kind of modernity from below as a political project: "I am polemically *opposed* to the notion that capitalism, because it has articulated modernity over the span of history so far, must go on doing so. It must be possible for people to conceive of themselves as of the present and of the future, that is to say *modern*, in ways that are not inscribed . . . by the imprint of capital."[14]

THREE

By the time he became a postgraduate in 1954, Hall had already moved out of the Oxford college into a student house on Richmond Road run by an American couple, Gerry and Beth Bentley.

Liberated from life in college, Hall started playing the piano again, joining a jazz group with a Barbadian student on the bass, a Jamaican bus driver who played drums and another Jamaican, also working on Oxford transport, who played the sax. He practised on an old piano in the basement of the house where he lived and played with the band at gatherings when invited. For a while, they had a regular Friday-night gig at a local cafe. This kind of "class crossing" – he was a middle-class intellectual, after all – was highly unusual among the Halls' social peers but it signalled his fundamentally egalitarian outlook, his refusal of the elite position to which he was entitled.

Music was important to Hall. Listening to his brother George's records, blues and jazz music in particular, had provided him with solace in Jamaica and he had learned to play the piano there. George was mainly interested in big-band swing – the music of Artie Shaw, Count Basie, Duke

Ellington and others. His closest school friends were also jazz aficionados and one of them introduced him to musicians such as Charlie Parker, Dizzy Gillespie, Thelonious Monk, Miles Davis, Kenny Clarke and Django Reinhardt.

Miles Davis was a particular favourite. In his later years, he would say that in his teens Davis had put a finger on his soul. *The Stuart Hall Project*, John Akomfrah's groundbreaking film about the cultural theorist, opens to music by Miles Davis, with Hall talking about what Davis's music meant to him and how the various moods of Miles Davis matched the evolution of his own feelings.

What Hall loved was the formal complexity of modern jazz, its fluidity and adventurous improvisation. Dancing to the "cooler rhythms" of jazz was different from dancing to mento, calypso or salsa – it was like "relaxing into the groove". Moreover, what he really loved about jazz was "the unbearable emotional depths the music seemed able to plumb without yielding an inch to sentimentality" (*Familiar Stranger*, 129). Its emotional intensity appealed to his conflicted self as a teenager.

Jazz was an emergent form of music in the 1940s and 1950s, its experimental nature and its roots in black American culture offering Hall and others like him growing up in the micro-islands of the Caribbean an alternative, counter-European modernity that spoke directly to them. "I always knew modern jazz was essentially a black voice," he would say (*Familiar Stranger*, 130) and it helped him find an alternative route to what Fanon had called "the fact of blackness".

The poet Kamau Brathwaite, who grew up in Barbados, mentions a similar relationship to jazz, describing it as an alternative to the European tradition. Jazz offered "a language to articulate the modernist impulse – of alienation, disillusionment and yet hope";[15] in doing so, it captured the dissonance felt by these budding young intellectuals in the colonial cultures they came from.

Certainly, the future was something that concerned Hall and his contemporaries. The lyrical freefall of jazz compositions by Miles Davis, Thelonious Monk and others presented a model of modernity that he felt was available to him, an aesthetic that could belong to him, and one to which he wanted to belong.

Films were also a passion, and Hall watched two to three films a week at Oxford, a carryover from his Kingston days when he would watch every film that came to town. In England, he was introduced to the work of Russian filmmakers and films from the continent, theatres in Kingston having been dominated by Hollywood. All these pursuits, literary criticism, reading modern literature both Caribbean and American, and playing jazz, constituted the construction of an "intellectual counter life" to the one available at the venerable English university.

The modernist movement in literature was also of interest to Hall but the staid Oxford curriculum did not accommodate much that was modern. With his burgeoning interest in culture, society and politics, the strictly literary occupied him less and less, so that instead of studying individual writers, Hall's focus shifted to the idea of modernity itself and the politics of modernism. He was also increasingly occupied by the social and historical context of literary studies.

Hall had once cherished notions of becoming a writer himself. Thus during his undergraduate years he had tried his hand at writing fiction and poetry, but despite having a couple of poems published in *Bim*, the Barbadian literary magazine, and another few acquired by the BBC's *Caribbean Voices* radio programme, he felt unable to write with conviction. There was a chasm between himself, born and bred in the colonial outpost of Jamaica, and the English. No matter how well he applied himself to the curriculum at Oxford, he felt he would never have the connotative context or the cultural codes required to convincingly represent the world as he knew it in fiction.

Keep in mind that young Hall felt doubly alienated, growing up middle class in colonial Jamaica, where there was a similar chasm between himself and members of the working classes. One obstacle would have been a linguistic one, with Hall only speaking the Queen's English while his black, working-class compatriots spoke a fluent patois, now called Jamaican or just Patwa, which he struggled to acquire.

Unlike jazz, to which he could relate directly and emotionally, connecting with modern poetry and other art forms was complicated. In poetry, the slippage between standard English, the pronunciation thereof, and the Jamaican vernacular seemed to present an insurmountable barrier. All the same, he did try his hand at writing a version of *King Lear* in Jamaican idiom.

In an attempt at a short story, Hall quite eloquently captured the essence of his linguistic dilemma:

People doan grow like plantain, the old folk used to say. You can't plant dem like yams. Whatever that meant. They had a way of talking as if the fruit of the soil had taken root in their tongues. Sum folks grow like vegetable, dey swell up and bus' like turnip: sum only good fe turn back in de soil. Sum yu' haf fe weed an' fork, but dey grow ripe and full like banana. Dey got all kin' a people: like dey got all kin' a fruit an' all kin' a ground.[16]

Identity seemed inextricably linked to language and Hall's inability to access the language of the people set him, irrevocably, he felt, apart:

It was a speech he knew, for they spoke it instinctively, as they shelled peas: but he couldn't speak it that way, for the language of the land had never taken root in his tongue, and he knew it now by proxy, by adoption. Grown on the edge of a City he had never thought of as such, couldn't visualise whole, although he knew it well, as even now he could visualise the London or New York he had never seen, his speech was slick and smooth and brassy like copper pennies. Well, he had grown, and time would tell whether he "just grewed" like plantain.

In his memoir, he talks of this linguistic identity crisis. Although he would never speak the language of his land, he eventually did find a vernacular he could live with: "It was only years later that I felt at home in language again – when I had managed to lose the Oxford cadences which had crept uninvited into my speech, and somehow unconsciously relearned to speak more conversationally, with rather than at an audience, in the rhythm of my own feelings, in a more relaxed, vernacular style" (*Familiar Stranger*, 172).

Meanwhile, there remained the question of his writing

voice. Hall despaired that he would ever find a fictional voice that rang true. It was a despondency familiar to many a young colonial, and even postcolonials. A younger Jamaican writer, Michelle Cliff, captured the predicament well: "The Anglican ideal – Milton, Wordsworth, Keats – was held before us with an assurance that we were unable, and would never be able, to achieve such excellence. We crouched outside the cave."[17]

Despite having gone to Jamaica College, painstakingly patterned after an English public school – the playing field of Imperial Man, as he called it – Hall felt unable to tune in to the innate Englishness those born in the country could access. As he later wrote, he lacked the "tacit knowledges", the cultural equivalent of what the French linguist Saussure called *langue* that the English could take for granted: "I was excluded from sharing a habitus – a way of life, forms of customary behaviour, a structure of common sense, taken-for-granted assumptions, affective identifications and presuppositions about the society, and how things work, below the conscious or purely cognitive level" (*Familiar Stranger*, 205).

Lacking the requisite perceptual or shared codes of meaning, Hall felt unable to tune into the richer symbolic, metaphorical or connotative aspects of English cultural practices. He explained this at length in his memoir: "Connotative contexts of meaning offer pictures of the world, rules of interpretation, a set of unspoken background assumptions, non-rational discursive logics, 'taken-for-granteds', pleasures and sentiments which constitute the semantic *langue* of a culture." He found himself unable to write from within English culture, gradually feeling relegated to being a voyeur or an observer "conducting a permanent native eth-nography" (*Familiar Stranger*, 208–9).

In England, one of the things that baffled Hall was "the contrast between the ordinariness – dreariness, even – of much of everyday life and the certainty possessed by the English of their exalted place in the world" (*Familiar Stranger*, 214). To what did they owe their innate, unspoken, taken-for-granted assumption of natural superiority, he wondered.

The acute awareness of his dislocation and distance from the inner world of the English strengthened Hall's critical faculties rather than his creative ones, which he could feel gradually atrophying. "I felt excluded at exactly the deep level where, for me at that moment, creative writing began" (*Familiar Stranger*, 209). He felt that, as a result, his writing voice was inauthentic, derivative. And being a writer, he tried to articulate these feelings, albeit often through a fictional alter ego:

> He had always thought it would come naturally, inevitably, as it seemed to do for Shakespeare: to thrust the blank square sheet of paper between roller and keys was a gesture towards composition as dramatic in its own right – perhaps more so – than putting quill to parchment. But a certain hesitancy of utterance, which was also a hesitancy of spirit, a cringing away from the very act of commitment, of involvement, which was inherent in creation, had shadowed him all of his life. His diffidence faced him now with a grim clarity. Nothing but the arbitrary act of the creative will, emotion and word falling together as if in some spontaneous shape, some specific epiphany, lay between him and composition. But it was a gorge as deep and treacherous as it was narrow.[18]

Hall was expressing the diffidence of many a would-be writer from what were considered the provinces, the periphery:

> And faced there with his own reluctance, his own timidity to commit feeling and passion, naked as an unsheathed sword – faced there with his own peculiar brand of cowardice, lurking in the corner of a soul, not expansive but ample, not accomplished but ambitious, he felt again the sudden clutch of fear, the sharp sense of a self-imposed silence, of a narrow but fertile talent spent almost in the very act of contemplating its own poverty.

Nevertheless, the handful of poems and stories Hall left behind are not as bad as he imagined they were. They display a highly developed social consciousness and a flair for turning a phrase. They are also suffused with the pain of indecision about returning to Jamaica. The theme of departure, leaving home to venture out into the world on his own, was clearly on his mind, as can be seen in the following excerpt from an inconclusive short piece of fiction where he wrote his anguish into his protagonist's thoughts:

> Well, sometimes a man had to go: sometimes, before the storm came, or work dried up, by the end of the planting, a man had to sell-out, close up shop and move out. A man had to get out or be damned. The sea was a long watery farewell, and a journey was a way to cut the last cords, to splice the navel, and be gone into the world. Sometimes a man, even a young man, had to shuffle the pack and deal himself a new hand. Somewhere out there, beyond the darkness where the seas stopped, a new world waited, and it couldn't be too quick before they drew up cable

and nosed out of the harbour. Others could come back if they wanted, others who were braver than he could come back to that long dockside and the low-slung warehouses and listen to that damn chanting as they loaded fruit. This was the last time he would hear it.

In a preceding excerpt, young Hall had depicted a dockyard scene of banana-loaders, wailing work chants like litanies, while lined up to convey their heavy loads into the ship's hold. The shambolic nature of emancipation from slavery, and independent nationhood haunted him: he felt that the formerly enslaved had been dealt a bad hand, one they did not have the luxury of reshuffling to deal themselves a better one. They were stuck with the hand they had been dealt.

The banana loaders were doing work that was hardly different from what their forebears had been doing a century ago. Added to the misery brought on by his ineluctable family circumstances, the slavery-like conditions of the working class had hardened Hall's determination to escape and create a better life somewhere else

In another short story, the young protagonist Scott's reflections are plainly an expression of the angst Hall himself was feeling:

> The question, of course, that faced him at last, was where in fact he did belong, what, in reality, he was: . . . and how much he was what the past had made him, what his father and his family and their expectations – what they all had fated him to be, before he took a step or uttered a cry, what the dumb past that spoke only with other voices, other accents, other hopes for him, demanded that he should be. He wondered at the

forces that had chained him into this circle of class and connection, that he could not break free from, even if that was his only wish, even if that was the very condition of his continuing to exist.

Could Hall deal himself a new hand? It is obvious that in his fiction, he was working out his own conflicted feelings about returning to Jamaica now that his sojourn at Oxford was coming to an end. Born into the family that he was, there would be no escaping his emplacement, as far as he was concerned, on the wrong side of the social landscape. He knew that if he returned, his life would be circumscribed by "a thousand expectations and unexplained loyalties that threaten to engulf him from the past, from whose pressing obligation he had no desire, except to be free" ("The Strike").

Years later, in a 2012 video interview, Hall was asked if he missed living in Jamaica. His response was matter of fact and echoed what his fictional alter ego had said sixty years earlier:

> I don't miss being embedded in the brown middle class of Jamaica. I think they colonized independence for themselves. And hundreds of thousands of Jamaicans are still left outside of that. I don't miss that at all. I don't miss the extraordinary entrepreneurialism that has taken hold of Jamaica. You know I go back to Jamaica and I turn on the radio expecting to hear that wonderful accent and all I'm hearing about is how stocks and shares have gone up.

Shedding the orthodoxies of Oxford in the midst of his identity crisis and deciding to stay in England, Hall experienced his "rebirth" as a diasporic subject: "From a diasporic position, I was privileged to see a past I knew well in the process of unravelling, and a future emerging whose shape I could not foresee but in which I would be a participant" (*Familiar Stranger*, 172).

He called this the "third space", the diasporic space, a fluid, ever-evolving space always in transit along with those who inhabit it. Unstable migratory populations gave rise to cultures that were unpredictable and contingent, as the marginal merged with the core. "In a suitably paradoxical formulation, displacement moved to the centre of things," said Hall in his memoir (*Familiar Stranger*, 62). Years later, speaking of the realities of retranscription and resignification that living in the diaspora forces, Hall urged his audience at the 1996 Rex Nettleford conference in Kingston, Jamaica to consider "a notion of the diasporic which lives with the notion of dissemination, of the scattering. The seed has gone out. It is not going to come back to its original ecology. It has to learn to resist pests that it never resisted before."[19]

FOUR

all spent his postgraduate years from 1954 on, informally studying and trying to understand the nature of Caribbean culture, its complex entanglement with Britain and Africa, the complicated processes of creolization arising out of slavery and colonialism and his own relationship to the continuing consequences of this historical formation. He was supposed to be studying English literature but the conjuncture he found himself at was shifting his attention elsewhere.

The black presence in England spurred Hall on to study how his compatriots were adapting and surviving the hostile conditions. In 1948 the *Empire Windrush* brought 1,027 passengers, mostly men, from Trinidad and Jamaica to England. It was the beginning of a migration that would last intermittently until 1962, bringing a total of ninety-eight thousand migrants from the Caribbean to the United Kingdom.

Hard times had befallen the Caribbean after World War II, and those who had fought for Britain and returned home found little to keep them there. Many took advantage of the thousands of berths available on the troop-decks at twenty-eight pounds per passenger and gladly returned to England, where postwar labour shortages had created a demand for workers to help rebuild the war-devastated country. For others this was their first encounter with the less than welcoming mother country.

Hall had decided to stay in England and become part of the Caribbean diaspora, but he realized that to survive he needed to create a stake for himself in British society while taking care not to be "assimilated" into it. This prompted a deeper engagement with British politics and trying to figure out how British society worked with a view to changing and transforming it.

The early 1950s were full of the political fallout of the Cold War – the West's fight against the spread of communism from the East and the polarization of the world into two rival socio-economic blocs. Already an ardent anti-colonialist, Hall was radicalized even further by the events of these years. Back in the Caribbean, the effects of US intervention into the region were being felt along with continuing British imperialism.

In 1952 the purging of "communists" from the leadership of the People's National Party in Jamaica under the heavy hand of US foreign policy was followed in April 1953 by the election of Cheddi Jagan's multi-ethnic Marxist-leaning People's Progressive Party to the government in British Guiana. By October 1953, the British had overthrown Jagan in a military operation, suspending British Guiana's constitution, firing its legislators and arresting Cheddi Jagan and his wife Janet.

Shortly thereafter we find Hall commenting on the situation in British Guiana with the assurance of a seasoned analyst. He was all of twenty-three years of age, but in an unpublished essay titled "The Social and the National Revolutions" he launched into a vigorous critique of British socialists, accusing them of resorting to platitudes instead of searching for the realpolitik at stake in the situation of colonial countries. Nationalism was not always coterminous with socialism in the colonies:

> Nationalism is not by definition "Progressive". The evolution of national leaders to power does not necessarily guarantee a change in the social and economic structure. It is my belief that nationalism can be a dangerously regressive force . . . the lesson which socialists might well learn is that the social revolution and the National revolution in colonial societies may overlap in personnel, but that the two movements are not necessarily coterminous. If the National revolution in a colonial society were to succeed and were to bring to power – economic and political power – a fully "prepared" colonial bourgeoisie, such as exists in the West Indies, there is no guarantee that there would be any major change in society.

It was time, Hall went on, for British socialists to stop placing their confidence and trust in native leaders, simply because they were native and nationalist, and time they began to consider the social goals which motivated different nationalist leaders:

> When Asia presses on the front page of the popular press, and Africa presses on the centre, the West Indies tend to find themselves relegated to the status of the advertisements on the

back page. The fact is that socialists don't quite know what to make of us. . . . Let me put it in terms of British Guiana. The British interests are maintained in British Guiana at the point of rifles and at the current expense of democratic forms of representation, *not* because the British people are a wicked race determined to stamp on the faces of happy natives. They are there because of the interests of British and American invested capital, and because a dissident territory on the South American mainland would seriously threaten the soft underbelly of the United States, would threaten the only channel between Britain and Australia, if Egypt and the Middle East were to prove recalcitrant about the Suez Canal and because it would disrupt the carefully prepared strategic structure of American military defence in Latin America.[20]

Hall also recalled celebrating the defeat of the French in Vietnam in 1954 at a Chinese restaurant with Doddridge Alleyne. It was a heady moment, according to historian Jean-Pierre Rioux, "the only pitched battle to be lost by a European army in the history of decolonisation".[21] These events led up to the Bandung Conference in 1955 and the dream of creating a "third force" to defuse the Cold War.

If Hall felt crippled by his cultural background when it came to literary writing there was no such diffidence about wading into political commentary. In a 1955 essay titled "The West Indies in the World", he produced a sophisticated assessment of the global geopolitical situation and of where and how the proposed federated West Indies should position itself.

"The economic depression which ravaged the metropolitan powers between 1929 and 1933 hit the West Indies later in the decade, between 1935 and 1937," he declared, going on to list the political repercussions in countries "responsible for the management of their own affairs". In the colonial West Indies, in the absence of self-government, the situation, as Hall described it, was quite different:

> In the West Indies, trade suffered, and unemployment rose alarmingly. But there were no immediate so-called "political" consequences: no governments fell, for there were none to fall. In this sense, in spite of labour unrest, the West Indies were cushioned and protected from an international crisis with which, so far as the conscious taking of policy was concerned, they were not involved. Yet in spite of this, the effects of the depression in the West Indies were far-reaching. The labour agitation between 1935 and 1937, which led to the appointment of the Moyne Commission, was the first mass movement which may be said to have been "Caribbean" in scope and character. It was responsible for the growth of trade unionism in the area and marks the emergence of a political consciousness in the region. These years may be considered the cradle years of West Indian nationalism.

Hall then moved on to discuss what he described as the next major international crisis – the declaration of war against Germany in 1939. By virtue of being colonies, the West Indies were involved, ipso facto, in the hostilities, although at a remove. This meant that the effects of the war were radically different for each society: "The immediate con-sequences of the war for Britain were the disruption of the structure of her foreign-trade, the reduction in size of her markets, the decline in purchasing power of her coin, and the diminution of her stature as a world power, vis-a-vis America and the Soviet Union."

All this meant that Britain had to readjust to a complex new structure of power in the world while financing a social revolution at home and remaining economically viable. In the West Indies, on the other hand, the war gave the nationalist movements a boost, with revised patterns of colonial administration and increased recruitment of native talent into management and administration.

The breakup of the older systems of colonial empires and the evolution of new nation states occurred in the context of a rapid and continuous polarization of power between two armed blocs. According to Hall, the lesson such countries as India, Pakistan and Ceylon had to offer was that an independent foreign policy was impossible without *being* independent.

❦

The student house on Richmond Road where Hall lived was a communal hub, run as a collective by the students themselves. They ate communally, took turns at weekly cooking and shared the premises with itinerant students who needed shelter. When it was his turn to cook, Hall tried to reproduce the food made by his family's cook, Ethel, on their old wood stove, employing the spices she would have used to produce the creole cuisine of his childhood. This was where and when Hall finally came into himself, feeling independent and in charge of his own life at last.

Richmond Road was a locus of political activity and

intellectual argument. This was where the New Left was born and where Hall, along with three others, would found a journal named *Universities and Left Review* in 1957. Gabriel Pearson, Raphael Samuel and Charles (Chuck) Taylor, along with Hall, co-edited *Universities and Left Review*. The first two were members of the Communist Party, while Taylor was a French-Canadian Rhodes scholar. Hall, not a Stalinist, belonged to the Socialist Club, which kept its distance both from the Communist Party and the anti-communist Labour Party. The lively discussions and debates with like-minded young men and women stimulated Hall and he began to dis-engage more and more from Oxford, only going to college for tutorials.

There was a sense that debates such as the ones Hall and his fellow editors were engaged in were occurring at other universities too (despite the fact that universities in the 1950s were hardly hotbeds of activism). This led to the inclusion of "Universities" in the title of the new journal. The rest of the title was a hat-tip to the *Left Review*, a wide-ranging and unor-thodox literary and cultural journal of the 1930s and 1940s, more receptive to new cultural movements (for example, in its openness to modernist currents), according to Hall, than any comparable "party" journal of its time.

A parallel journal called the *New Reasoner*, based in Yorkshire, was started by the Communist Party Historians Group, and included scholars such as E.P. Thompson and Eric Hobsbawm. Eventually these two journals were consolidated into the *New Left Review*, with Hall as its first editor.

The *Reasoners* were suspicious of the London-based

Universities and Left Review and the cosmopolitan left-wingers associated with it. Although there were important differences between them, the coalition survived but the New Left was never monolithic or culturally and politically homogeneous.

Life in the Richmond Road collective was tumultuous, with Gabriel, Raphael and Hall preoccupied with bringing *Universities and Left Review* out in addition to the rigours of daily life. Correcting proofs around the dinner table, cooking for themselves and cleaning up, and looking after the itinerant friends who took up residence with them were all time-consuming but immensely satisfying activities.

Chuck Taylor became Hall's unofficial mentor, especially in matters of high philosophy. Another close friend was Alan Hall, whom he met in 1952 when the Scottish scholar first came to Oxford. Alan was an archaeologist and active in the early New Left. The two explored the Labour Club at Oxford, the student branch of the Labour Party and even attended a few Communist Party meetings, although Hall steadfastly refused to join the party. By 1956 he and Alan had plans to write a book on the fractures beginning to show in British culture and politics, but this never materialized.

The New Left emerged out of a profound generational shift within the Marxist Left between those who attempted to fit the world into a narrow, mechanistic Marxist framework privileging the economic base of society over what was considered the superstructure or secondary effects of the economic mode of production. Young scholars and activists like Hall thought the Marxist toolbag as it existed was inadequate to explain the huge cultural changes British society had experienced in the wake of the war. For them, traditional Marxist tools of analysis were simply not complex or sensitive enough to grasp the new realities of affluence and full capitalist immersion.

Thus it was that Hall began to turn increasingly away from literature towards the historical, social and political questions of the time. Unable to identify with any of the traditional Left political parties or tendencies, Hall and his friends tried to come up with a less rigid and reductionist form of Marxism, less dependent on the economy as the privileged interpretive window into human existence. Like Althusser, Hall refused to believe that "His Majesty the Economy can detach itself from its political, ideological and cultural conditions of existence and dictate on its own".[22]

In 1956 two major events shook Hall's world and made him rethink his political positions. First, the declaration of war on Egypt by Britain, France and Israel in retaliation for Nasser's seizing of the Suez Canal; second, the invasion of Hungary by the Soviet Union and the brutal put-down of the popular anti-Stalinist revolution there by Stalin's troops. The urgency of finding a new politics he could live with weighed on Hall and the events of 1956 forever shaped his political thinking, turning him against hard-line Marxism.

The invasion of Hungary had driven a wedge between Marxists who supported Stalin's tactics and those who were repelled by what seemed to them to be nothing short of a fascist suppression of Hungarians. Following Britain's militaristic response to Egypt's nationalization of the Suez Canal later the same year, the world became locked in a crisis that neither right-wing nor left-wing politics seemed able to tackle. It was what Hall would famously call a conjuncture – an emergent constellation of historically specific events, predicaments and ideological circumstances producing a crisis or political cul-de-sac.

In late 1956, only a day or two before the Soviet invasion of Hungary, a New Left group including Hall travelled to London to take part in a huge anti-Suez demonstration. It was Hall's first big mass political demonstration, where he experienced first-hand the repressive powers of the state. There were those who felt that the readiness of Britain to orchestrate an invasion of Egypt inspired Stalin to invade Hungary. Hall, who had always remained far from the Oxford Union, was moved to take part in the debate held there on the Suez crisis.

The invasion of Hungary precipitated the search by the young Oxford students for a more humane socialism, for a third space where people could be involved, whatever their affiliations, in independent political activity and debate. The *Universities and Left Review* and the *New Reasoner* were not merely journals, they were also the organs of incipient political movements.

But Hall's first "proper" political essay was on the self-destruction of Anthony Eden following his 1956 declaration of war on Egypt.[23] It was Hall's first attempt at conjunctural analysis, anticipating his 1979 intervention "The Great Moving Right Show". Curiously, with the colonial web still firmly in place, Jamaica was very much part of Eden's downward spiral, showing the continuing entanglement of outpost with empire. When Eden disappeared after the Americans put a stop to his aggression on Egypt, it was to Jamaica he escaped to recover and save face. It was a fine demonstration of what Hall described as the troubled flows and interconnections between Caribbean colonial societies and the imperial metropolis over several centuries.

The *Daily Gleaner* of 25 November 1956 had a banner headline all in uppercase, "EDEN COMES FOR REST". The British couple had arrived the previous day on a BOAC jet named *Seven Seas* and were greeted by a band singing "Jamaica the Garden of Eden Welcomes Britain's Sir Anthony Eden".

During Eden's absence from England, matters took their own course, with the *Spectator* commenting that Jamaica had done more damage than Suez to Sir Anthony's standing in his party at Westminster. In his absence the Conservative Party met in secret caucus and it was decided that when Anthony Eden returned to England he would be asked to resign. Three weeks after his return, he was ousted from office. It was the beginning of the end of empire, if not imperialism.

In a 2010 *New Left Review* article, Hall wrote about the conjunctural significance of 1956, the fact that it marked a turning point after which the world would never seem – or be – the same:

> The "first" New Left was born in 1956, a conjuncture – not just a year – bounded on one side by the suppression of the Hungarian Revolution by Soviet tanks and on the other by the British and French invasion of the Suez Canal zone. These two events, whose dramatic impact was heightened by the fact that they occurred within days of each other, unmasked the

underlying violence and aggression latent in the two systems that dominated political life at the time – Western imperialism and Stalinism – and sent a shock wave through the political world. In a deeper sense, they defined for people of my generation the boundaries and limits of the tolerable in politics. Socialists after "Hungary", it seemed to us, must carry in their hearts the sense of tragedy which the degeneration of the Russian Revolution into Stalinism represented for the left in the twentieth century. "Hungary" brought to an end a certain kind of socialist innocence. On the other hand, "Suez" underlined the enormity of the error in believing that lowering the Union Jack in a few ex-colonies necessarily signalled the "end of imperialism", or that the real gains of the welfare state and the widening of material affluence meant the end of inequality and exploitation. "Hungary" and "Suez" were thus liminal, boundary-marking experiences. They symbolized the break-up of the political Ice Age.[24]

FIVE

The years between 1956 and 1964 for Hall were dominated by political activity, editing *Universities and Left Review* and, from 1960, *New Left Review*. Hall was one of the chief architects of the New Left, which now attempted to coalesce through a mass movement organized around the dismantling of Britain's status as a nuclear superpower. With the division of the world into two opposing camps armed with nuclear weapons, the threat of nuclear war loomed large and particularly concerned Hall, who started participating in demonstrations and campaigns to counter nuclear arms and energy. After attending the first Campaign for Nuclear Disarmament (CND) Aldermaston March in 1958, disarmament became Hall's primary focus for the next few years. He later became an activist and speaker for the CND, touring the countryside and putting his declamatory skills to good use.

Hall's extraordinary political voice was in evidence at the CND rallies in Trafalgar Square at the end of the Aldermaston marches in the late 1950s and early 1960. Most speakers were predictable, but not Hall: he was possessed of a beautiful, sonorous voice and he was able to bring thought and feeling together memorably. The London New Left Club, of which Hall was a founding member, was a prominent supporter of the first CND Aldermaston March. This was the beginning of close links between the New Left and the CND, which was emerging as a mass political organization.

Hall authored two pamphlets for the CND, one attempting a political critique of NATO and of the NATO alliance. The second pamphlet outlined the policy of "positive neutralism" espoused by Hall and members of the New Left, in which they refused to choose between the two nuclear camps, looking instead towards the newly decolonized and independent states of the world as a strategic, alternative force in the global arena.

In 1958 Hall had moved from Oxford to London, where he started working as a supply teacher at the Stockwell Secondary Modern School, remaining there until 1960. Though it was a predominantly white, working-class school, supply teachers were often foreigners – Australians, West Indians, Indians, Pakistanis. While teaching there, he lived in the home of Jock and Millie Haston, a Trotskyite Glaswegian seaman and his South African wife.[25] Despite the congenial living circumstances, the move to London was a difficult, lonely transition for Hall which he countered with his active involvement in editorial and political work:

> I got a job in a secondary school as a supply teacher, and you're sent round to different schools, but my school was unable to retain any of its supply teachers, or indeed its teachers. So once I'd got in there they never let me go. I was a supply teacher in a school at the Kennington Oval, for quite a while, about three

or four years, and I used to leave there, get on a train, go to Soho, and edit the journal, and go back on the night bus – try to wake up in time to get to the Oval for the opening of class.[26]

Even today supply teachers earn lower pay, fewer benefits and have too little support compared to salaried full-time teaching staff. The second tier of secondary modern schools was reserved for working-class children who had failed to get into the elite grammar schools. Although Hall loved teaching, he found his stint as a supply teacher a harrowing experience. He was very young, with no experience of teaching, but despite this was given a class of pupils who were repeaters and had little ambition but to follow in their fathers' footsteps as labour for local industries. The problem, thought young Hall, lay in secondary modern education itself: "It is ridiculous to talk of economic prosperity working, in the natural course of events, to break down established barriers between social classes. Class distinctions based upon attitudes, taste, education, and rooted in the educational system itself, do not wither away any more quickly than the State Department. A common culture does not 'just grow' out of a socially differentiated society, any more than grass roots flourish in stone."[27]

In 1954 Hall had given a paper on class in contemporary capitalism, a critique of orthodox Marxist analysis, to a discussion group set up by Raphael Samuel.[28] This led to Hall's important 1958 article "A Sense of Classlessness", published in the *Universities and Left Review*, where he attempted to take stock of the immense transformations occurring in postwar British society:

> In the area of south London where I live, old and new physical
> environments coexist within a single borough. Here are the old
> two-storey brick dwellings of a working-class suburb, row after
> row in a dark street butting straight into the warehouse, lumber
> yard or factory gate: there are the new eight-storey flats of an
> L.C.C. housing estate, enclosed in a grass-and-concrete jig-saw,
> offering the beginnings of a "contemporary" urban facade.
> Along the Brixton Road, the barrow boys are hawking goods
> outside a "utility" style British version of the super-market.
> Some of the local children go to school at a Dickensian brick
> building constructed – and hardly re-touched – since the
> 1880's: but not far away is the glass-and-steel compound of the
> local Comprehensive, not yet completed.[29]

After describing the physical changes in his neighbourhood, Hall goes on to discuss other fundamental changes
taking place because "post-war prosperity and the high levels
of employment have made possible new spending habits
amongst working people". There was a sea change in the
attitude of working-class people towards a range of consumer
goods, with many of them now able to contemplate the
purchase of cars and other items once considered luxuries for
workers like themselves. Thus a new style of urban life was
coming into being, induced by the spread, among other
things, of hire-purchase sales plans. This was "of course, one
way of stimulating a semi-stagnant economy: it is also,
however, an attempt – on the part of the Banks and Finance
Houses who are best equipped to do so – to catch up with and
sustain a current of domestic spending on furniture, household goods and appliances, TV sets, which has been growing,
with certain lapses, since the war".[30]

In fleshing out his argument, Hall turns to Raymond Williams, whose statement "the working class does not become bourgeois by owning the new products, any more than the bourgeois ceases to be bourgeois as the objects he owns change in kind" was particularly relevant.[31] Yet, argued Hall, it would be a mistake to dismiss the structural and institutional transformations as simply the result of a postwar boom. There was nothing temporary about the changes in social attitudes the working class were experiencing, as a result of having been "seduced into playing a complementary role to capitalism". The most significant change was the transition from being mere producers of labour to consumers of the very goods the "alienated labour" of the workers had created.

Hall's remarkable ability to read his own time, to focus on the present conjuncture – indeed, to historicize the present – was well in evidence by the age of twenty-six, as his close critical reading of the postwar turn to consumerism and all that it implied indicates. At *New Left Review* Hall worked closely with E.P. Thompson and Raymond Williams, whom he considered his intellectual fathers. They were important friends and mentors whom he never felt equal to. He felt hugely privileged when Williams gave Hall and his co-editor two draft chapters of what was to become his classic text, *Culture and Society,* for feedback. Hall had a more uneasy relationship with Ed Thompson, who, though a strong anti-imperialist, did not understand race, something that was increasingly occupying him.

Indeed, in 1958 it was impossible to ignore race in Britain. The steady influx of Caribbean immigrants who settled in and around communities such as Notting Dale and Notting Hill had aroused the ire of the impoverished white working-class people who lived there. The black immigrants were seen by poor whites as a threat to their jobs, their housing and their women. Tensions were simmering all year and came to a head in the summer when nine white youths – Teddy Boys – armed with iron bars, blocks of wood, an air pistol and a knife embarked on what they called a "nigger-hunting expedition" around Notting Hill. Five black men ended up in hospital, three severely wounded, as a result of the attacks.

But it was a public argument between a young Swedish woman, Majbritt, and her Jamaican husband, Raymond Morrison, that proved to be the catalyst for what would become known at the time as the White Riots of 1958,[32] the worst racial violence ever experienced in Britain up to that point. Soon enough, a white mob descended on the scene, attempting to defend Majbritt from her husband. She had not solicited their help but fighting started when Raymond's West Indian friends came to his rescue. By the next day a jeering two-hundred-strong white mob was at large waving sticks and butcher's knives, shouting "Down with the niggers!" and "Go home, you black bastards!"

Police who tried to protect black residents were accused of being "nigger lovers" and became the target of abuse themselves. The motto "Keep Britain White" was being bandied about and the *Daily Mail* carried an article titled "Should We Let Them Keep Coming In?", calling for tighter immigration controls. It was like fanning the flames of intolerance and three days of nonstop rioting followed.

Finally, a group of Jamaicans and others decided to fight back, throwing Molotov cocktails at the menacing crowd of whites, who backed off. The West Indians started chasing them with machetes and meat cleavers, managing to do something the police had found impossible – check the onslaught of the hostile white mobs. Within two days the situation had calmed down and 108 people, mostly white, were arrested. Though many were injured, no one died ("White Riot: The Week Notting Hill Exploded", *Independent*, 28 August 2008).

The management of difference after West Indian migrants landed and began to live in the United Kingdom had given way and the government, incredibly, tried to downplay the racial side of things and portray the conflict as a clash between "ruffians, both coloured and white" – or, simply, hooliganism. Senior officials and police chiefs tried to present the riots in 1958 as a regular "law and order" issue to protect the government from international political embarrassment at a time when delicate negotiations were going on between them and the soon-to-be independent colonies. In addition, the riots occurred when the Conservative government of the time was pursuing a policy of open immigration to Britain from the Commonwealth to fill job shortages.

Jamaica's chief minister Norman Manley made a trip to London urging Jamaicans in Notting Hill to be patient. "Remember what the American Negroes have had to put up with. And remember that at last they are winning." The integration of black students into white American schools was underway at the time, a huge step forward in asserting their civil rights and liberties for American blacks. Manley urged Jamaicans to stay indoors but to assert their civil rights at all times.

Hall noted that "hooliganism" was being vividly associated with "youth culture", such that, "In its famous editorial 'Hooliganism is Hooliganism', *The Times* mapped the Notting Hill events directly, not into the problem of race or of urban poverty, but into the problem of hooliganism, teenage violence, lawlessness, anarchy, together with the football spectator . . . and the railway carriage breaker. . . . 'All', *The Times* said, 'are manifestations of a strand of our social behaviour that an adult society can do without'" (*Selected*, 148).

The Notting Hill race riots were to be Hall's "first lesson in black diasporic politics". He became involved through the *Universities and Left Review* in the Notting Hill events, and the politics thereof. The New Left Club in London also became deeply involved with the anti-racist struggles of the period around North Kensington. As a supply teacher in south London, Hall often walked black pupils home from school to prevent them being attacked:

> We participated in the efforts to establish tenants' associations in the area, helped to protect black people who, at the height of the "troubles", were molested and harassed by white crowds in an ugly mood between Notting Hill station and their homes, and picketed Mosley and National Front meetings. . . . In the course of this work we first stumbled across the powerful traces of racism inside the local Labour Party itself, and Rachel Powell, an active club member, unearthed the scandal of "Rachmanism" and white landlord exploitation in Notting Hill.[33]

During this period, Hall met Michael de Freitas (better known as Michael X, a persona he adopted later),[34] a sort of strong-arm man or street hustler who worked for the notorious slum landlord Peter Rachman. De Freitas was employed by Rachman to throw black families out of their homes for owing rent. Hall met the man who would become known as Michael X when he came to the New Left Club. Passionate about jazz, Michael would go to Stockholm on weekends to hear American jazz bands. After interacting with Hall and his Left Club contemporaries, Michael X even switched to the side of the tenants he used to once harass, but in 1972 was convicted of murder in Trinidad and Tobago, where he had started a commune, and hanged in 1975. "This is why I think Michael X is a tragedy," said Hall, "because he had exactly the same formation as Malcolm X, who was from exactly the same hustling background; and Malcolm became something and Michael lost his way" (*Essential Essays*, 2:280).

In 1957 an important figure entered Hall's life. Michael Rustin (later to become Hall's brother-in-law) met him at a meeting of the New Left Club in 1957. Rustin was only in sixth form then. He recalls that while at Oxford, he was invited by Hall to go for a walk, during which he told him he had to write a philosophy essay on the subject "Are there universals?" Hall listened attentively and replied, "Perhaps there are", in a friendly but sceptical tone. It was an early indication of his lifelong interest in the particular, while his receptivity and ability to listen to others suggested that in another life he could have been a psychoanalyst. Hall's friendship and mentorship were a life-changing experience for Rustin, who later remarked the "exceptional inquiring intelligence" with which Hall met his complex experiences.

Also in the late 1950s, Hall met Paddy Whannel, a Scotsman, with whom he would go on to write an influential book, *The Popular Arts*, published in 1964. Whannel was with the British Film Institute and taught film long before it became the subject of study at the tertiary level. Hall and Whannel would often go to film societies to view foreign films that were not available in the local cinemas.

In 1962, Hall moved to Chelsea College, University of London, to teach film and "allied media" – television being considered too new and unworthy of academic attention at that stage to be included in a course title. Hall ended up lecturing for Whannel, teaching a course on gangster films, among other things. Whannel and Hall would tour the countryside giving lectures on popular culture. Hall even gave a lecture on westerns at Wandsworth Prison, something he enjoyed enormously, describing it as a "riot". On weekends, he and Paddy spent their time playing music and discussing popular culture at the Whannel home. The Whannel family offered a taste of family life, something Hall was by now, starved of:

> I used to spend Sundays with them, I used to spend Christmases with them and we simply looked at film, looked at magazines, listened to Billie Holiday, listened to Coleman Hawkins, listened to Ben Webster. He [Paddy] really introduced me to that generation of jazz players sort of just before the modern jazz. That was where his tastes lay. But he introduced me to it and we just talked about it. *The Popular Arts* grew out of these

intimate conversations while Paddy slowly absorbed a glass of whiskey and I would stay overnight and we'd read the Sunday papers and then we'd start again and we'd listen to Ben Webster and listen to Billie Holiday. It was the [sic] kind of personal feast, you know. And so we'd say, "Well, we'd better write some of this up because teachers would benefit from hearing this conversation, because they don't know how to talk about these things with their students." (*Personally Speaking*, 22)

Interestingly, *The Popular Arts* came out almost at the same time as *Understanding Media* by Marshall McLuhan, against which it was unfavourably compared especially by conservative commentators. McLuhan was the great media guru at the time and his theories were considered revolutionary in contrast to those put forward by the unknowns, Hall and Whannel. But in spite of the fact that McLuhan foresaw the advent of a World Wide Web–connected world thirty years ahead of the phenomenon, what Hall called his "technical determinism" did not stand the test of time, fading in importance by the 1970s.[35] Hall's ideas, on the other hand, have grown exponentially in relevance and value, becoming even more crucial to analysing twenty-first-century power relations than before.

A reviewer of *Popular Arts* noted that the teaching projects in the book "bring into play" the disciplines of history, sociology, psychology, and aesthetics. It is obvious from this that Hall was already well on his way to breaching disciplinary boundaries, a feature that was to become the hallmark of cultural studies, the field of inquiry synonymous with his name.

Hall's co-authorship of *The Popular Arts* led Richard Hoggart, founder-director of the now renowned Centre for Contemporary Cultural Studies at Birmingham University, to invite him to join the centre in 1964 as its first research fellow.[36]

Early work at the centre involved using the tools of literary criticism to analyse working-class culture and critique capitalism. Hoggart's *The Uses of Literacy* was a foundational text in what is called media studies today. Hoggart was also involved in adult education, using postwar reconstruction resources to educate members of the working class who were so inclined. Coming from a working-class background himself, Hoggart was well positioned to undertake such work.

The centre described itself as committed to the critical assessment of the social attitudes and cultural qualities of popular fiction, the press, films and television, popular music and advertising. Hall and the Birmingham Centre would go on to revolutionize attitudes towards popular culture globally, as well as traditional approaches to the study of humanities and social sciences, dismantling the disciplinary boundaries that compartmentalized human experience, knowledge and knowledge-gathering practices.

At a faculty seminar in 1999, Hall would elaborate on his commitment to interdisciplinarity:

> There are what I call "horses for courses". When the going is soft you need to know which jockey to put in the saddle. If you want detailed, scholarly, historical work, you don't put me in the saddle (laughs). I don't do it; I don't do it well. I don't know how it's done, and I don't have the patience for it. That is

because I came into cultural studies at the moment of its inter-disciplinarity. You can only do any work at all by thinking rather programmatically. To get embedded into any one discipline would exactly have been to let loose of the challenge of daring to think across the divide, although it's a kind of chasm. So I chose to go with the flow and to think across the divide, although the thinness of what that produces is a drawback.[37]

As Hall would later explain, Britain's very culture was in the throes of rapid change as the society was transformed from an old class society into a mass society by forces such as the advent of television and the rise of youth culture. The Fellows at the Birmingham Centre believed that school should be a place where students could reflect on life as they knew it, researching and studying the lives they were living and the things happening to them and around them.

In a BBC *Desert Island Discs* session (13 February 2000), Hall would say about the teaching practices of the Birming-ham Centre: "We were making it up as we went along. There was hardly a relationship of teacher and taught. They were my friends, my students, my apprentices." In a tribute to Hall in 2014, Kieran Connell and Matthew Hilton of the University of Birmingham noted Hall's intellectual generosity and the spirit of inquiry and debate that accompanied his and his colleagues' work. In contrast to most other intellectuals, he never published a monograph on his own. "His ideas were there to stimulate and provoke; to join a conversation that others would take up."[38]

Cultural studies was revolutionary because it had no fixed methodologies and was transdisciplinary verging on antidisciplinary. It was designed as a variable, flexible and critical mode of analysis that could be adapted to different contexts or conjunctures. Its signature was its lack of an easily codifiable, canonic set of rules and it resisted being seen as a "school" of thought. While at the Open University in the 1980s, Hall would say: "Codification makes my hackles rise, even about the things I have been involved in. . . . People talk about 'the Birmingham school' . . . and all I can hear are the arguments that we used to have in Birmingham that we never were one school; there may have been been four or five but we were never able to unify it all, nor did we want to create that kind of orthodoxy."[39]

Traditional elitist distinctions between high and low culture were to be avoided. Culture, ideology, language and the symbolic were all objects of study at the centre and Hall was instrumental in connecting with the work of French theorists such as Ferdinand de Saussure, Michel Foucault, Roland Barthes and others. But his main engagement was with the work of Antonio Gramsci, the Italian theorist of power relations.[40]

Hall was already thinking along the same lines as Gramsci long before he encountered the Italian activist's work, hence his enthusiastic adoption of the Gramscian approach. Applying Gramsci's model of hegemony and counter-hegemony to the analysis of political and social strife in Britain allowed cultural studies proponents to identify the ways in which the dominant culture served either to further social domination, or to enable people to resist and struggle against domination.

The series of co-written books, articles and working papers exploring a variety of topics such as subcultures (*Resistance Through Rituals*), race and the law (*Policing the Crisis*) and the theoretical aspects of cultural inquiry (*Culture, Media, Language*) that issued from the centre placed the University of Birmingham on the map in the 1970s.

In particular, *Policing the Crisis*, a seminal work, cemented Hall's reputation as a political and social analyst. Collaboratively produced with his colleagues and students, *Policing the Crisis* exemplified the Birmingham Centre's new approach to scholarship as well as providing a compelling application of Hall's encoding/decoding thesis and the "conjunctural analysis" that became his hallmark.

Policing the Crisis argued that a crisis-ridden UK government had tried to displace and channel growing social anxiety onto the bodies of young immigrant black men by creating a moral panic around street crime, now labelled "mugging". The post–World War II economic boom was petering out and the industrialized economies of North America and western Europe were sagging. Talk of the "affluent society" constructed during the consumer-driven boom of the 1950s and 1960s was waning while the race conflict in the United States was escalating, along with rising crime rates and the breakdown of law and order. Amid mutterings about a liberal conspiracy, it was what Hall and his colleagues would call, after Gramsci, a full-blown "organic crisis".[41]

In August 1972 a British newspaper reported on a violent robbery as "a mugging gone wrong". The importation of the term "mugging" from American media brought with it the association with race and the urban crisis in places like New York. In the United States, mugging was identified with black gangs.

What made *Policing the Crisis* such an important intervention was its self-announced attempt to sneak up on public opinion and capture it even as it was in the process of being formed. Nothing like that had been attempted before. "Looking conjuncturally enabled the authors to painstakingly map the trajectory of 'the mugger', his socio-cultural imprint becoming more firmly stamped on public consciousness with each repetition of mugger discourse, across news media, courtrooms, public commentary, everyday conversation, gossip and other formal and official sites of disquiet."[42]

Policing the Crisis essentially teased out and exposed the elaborate manufacture of public consent that had taken place in the United Kingdom in the late 1970s, enabling more invasive and authoritarian forms of policing, particularly against black immigrant communities, to creep in. Mainstream media's central role in orchestrating this state of affairs was laid bare along with the multifaceted and interdependent nature of the institutional response to crime.

Policing the Crisis showed the coordinated nature of responses from the police, the courts and the media, proving they were an integral part of constructing the panic, not just institutions independently reacting to a crisis. "These institutions get to decide which issues are highlighted, how crime statistics are interpreted, where police resources are allocated, and how they are given meaning in relation to the wider societal context. Which is not to say that institutions are completely in control of the dynamic, as in the end all of them are 'acting out a script they do not write'."[43]

The ensuing moral panic allowed the public to be distracted from the wider, more organic crisis the state found itself in, allowing authorities to clamp down and contain it. This is a strategy that has been replayed and continues to be used over and over again not only in Britain but all over the world. According to Hall, it was in response to these combined crises that the developed countries gradually articulated the hegemonic project now known as neo-liberalism. Neoliberalism included attacks on institutions of working-class power, shrinking the redistributive arm of the state, and bolstering the state's security apparatus. It was the beginning of what Hall termed "popular authoritarianism" and it heralded the arrival of a new political force in Britain, Margaret Thatcher.

Hall's deft analysis of Thatcher's rise to power and the ascent of the radical right in British corridors of power ("Thatcherism") that preceded her election in 1979 consolidated his position as a political sociologist and analyst par excellence. In an article titled "The Great Moving Right Show" (*Marxism Today*, January 1979), Hall demonstrated how Thatcher had unified into one political force several disparate, right-leaning interest groups, added labour interests who adhered to the "traditional values" the radical right considered important – family, nation, empire – and directed state power against those excluded from this formulation by race, ethnicity and political philosophy. The ensuing "authoritarian populism" proved to be tensile and muscular, mobilizing citizens against what it portrayed as a flabby welfare state that benefited immigrants, feminists and a legion of "others" the state could no longer afford to maintain at public expense, according to this increasingly popular neo-liberal world view. Hall concluded, "Thatcherism has found a powerful means of popularizing the principles of a monetarist philosophy; and, in the image of the welfare 'scavenger', a well-designed folk-devil" (*Selected*, 179).

Michael Rustin writes in the afterword to *Selected Political Writings* that *Policing the Crisis* remains insufficiently recognized as the exceptional piece of political analysis it was, identifying and anticipating as it did the contours of Thatcherism a full year before Margaret Thatcher became prime minister of Britain.

SIX

B ut what of Hall's personal life? Were there no liaisons, romantic or otherwise? During his student years in England, Hall occasionally had girlfriends and there are references to one in particular whom he met while teaching in Jamaica. Although she visited him at Oxford and afterwards, like various other relationships at the time, this one remained unresolved. Hall's political activities in the early years left little room for romantic relationships.

His life took a turn for the better during the turbulent 1960s. In 1963, on the CND march from Aldermaston to London, Hall met Michael Rustin's wife's sister, Catherine Barrett, who was seventeen at the time. It was a momentous meeting. Although Catherine was thirteen years Hall's junior and about to begin university, the two fell in love and got married in 1964.

Catherine had just begun a degree programme at Sussex when they met. After they married and Hall started his job as a research fellow at the Birmingham Centre, Catherine transferred to the University of Birmingham, where she studied history. Hall's first trip back to Jamaica was in 1965, a year after his wedding. The Halls took a boat both ways, a seven-week holiday that doubled as honeymoon. Hall presented his bride to his family but young Catherine soon found herself on the wrong side of the matriarch, Jessie, after objecting to her speaking ill of the household help in their presence.

Back home in Birmingham the Halls tried their best to settle down into family life. As a graduate student participating in student and university politics, Catherine became involved in the feminist movement and found it difficult juggling her academic career with being a young mother after Rebecca (Becky) and Jess, their daughter and son, were born.

The arrival of children made life for the Halls more hectic and complex. Becky came first, born 27 December 1968. Catherine went into labour on Christmas Day. Later Hall is reputed to have said that Becky's birth was well placed "but a little untimely", coming as it did so soon after the student sit-ins at Birmingham and just before a festive screening of *Some Like It Hot*, one of Hall's best-loved films.

Sit-ins had become a mode of protest at US universities in the late 1960s and in 1968 they caught on in the United Kingdom, where student upheavals had begun. The University of Birmingham sit-in of 1968 was about the right of students to participate in the decision-making process of the university. Five hundred students occupied the Great Hall of the university for about a week and although the Birmingham sit-in may not have registered on the global scale, it affected Hall, who, along with others at the centre, supported the protest.[44] This led to a troubled relationship with the university, ensuring he would never be promoted and investment in the centre was minimized. As Kieran Connell and Matthew Hilton observed, the centre achieved its remarkable output of empirical research and theoretical reflection in this period with a permanent staff of just two or three lecturers. Hall got the best out of his colleagues and raised the bar for what could be achieved by graduate students.

The sit-in had barely ended when Becky made her entrance, giving Hall a new identity to experience; it was one he relished, finding the experience of becoming a father "a wonder". Their son was born two years later. The children called him Grizzly Bear, but never feared asking him questions because their curiosity was always welcomed with a smile. As a small boy, Jess recalled being drawn to Hall's dark study by the rat-a-tat-tat of his typewriter and the smell of tobacco.

After Becky was born, Catherine became interested in the women's liberation movement and, along with others, started an early consciousness-raising group about women's experiences and identity. The division of labour in households around children, marriage, the right to birth control and abortion were some of the areas the group focused on. The areas of the young couple's intellectual work diverged in predictable directions: "The division of labour in our household was that Stuart worked on race, which meant black men, and I worked on gender, which meant white women: a variation on that common phenomenon on the Left, where men dealt with class and women with gender."[45]

Racism was rife in Birmingham and the Halls as an

interracial couple attracted hostility and had difficulty finding an affordable place to rent. When they finally settled down, Hall once again allowed his work to consume him, though he occasionally took time out to go dancing with Catherine and other friends. The Halls were close to the Rustins, Catherine's sister, Margaret, and her husband Michael.

For Margaret Rustin, Hall had been a name from the pages of the *New Statesman*, read avidly in their family home in Leeds. She eventually met him at Oxford through her husband Michael, and when Hall married her sister in 1964, it cemented their bond. The two families led intertwined lives, going on holidays with their children. They played vigorous outdoor games, including backyard cricket, though as Hall grew older he moved from playing in family games to being the referee.

The Birmingham years, with young children and Catherine first a student and then a young lecturer, were financially precarious ones for the Halls. Contact with the family back home in Jamaica had been sporadic and there had been few visits to the country as airfares were too expensive for their slim budget.

Hall did manage to send a little money home occasionally but his busy schedule did not permit him to write often. Catherine was the one who kept in touch with Hall's sister and other family members. After Hall's parents died, his sister, Patricia, who had looked after them as they aged, turned her attention to their older brother, George, who was completely blind by then.

Hall felt anguished at his sister's plight, at how the family had hijacked her life completely, denying her any chance at self-determination and happiness in her own right. She never worked again after the damaging interventions into her relationship with a young black medical student and the shock treatment "therapy" that followed. Nor did she ever have a romantic relationship again. To Hall, it seemed as if Patricia was suffering from the disease of colonialism. What bothered him was that in spite of the harm Pat suffered at the hands of the family, she still dedicated her life to caring for her aging parents and visually disabled brother. They became her life and she discharged her duties with dedication and resolve. Hall tried in vain to persuade Patricia to find a job, to get a life of her own, but she did not see how she could oblige him. Indeed, she did not seem to have the will to do so. In a handwritten letter dated 1982 she wrote:

> I'm a little disappointed to see that, in spite of all I've written about *our particular situation*, *you* are disappointed that I haven't found it possible to take part-time work. I've certainly tried to explain, in great detail, what the reasons are. Perhaps you don't have time to read what's written: Perhaps it's hard to visualize at such a distance. I'm sorry to think you choose to ignore the fact of George's handicaps, their implications, and what this all means in time and energy where I am concerned. Perhaps it's hard for you to understand that, at 62, George needs a great deal of day-to-day practical help, quite apart from the fact that he needs help with things to occupy him and keep his sanity.

The problems seemed endless. There isn't anyone else to look after George, explained Pat, "not that I succeed all that well". If she employed the kind of assistants competent to help with her brother, she could not earn enough to pay them as her health would not permit it. There are references to antidepressants, to a combined sinusitis, laryngitis and bronchitis attack earlier that year which "hit me for six". Pat complained of constant anxiety "about how to cope": "Of course the solution is to get a paid job. But *what* to do about George?? I can't even suggest sending him to you for the practical care and working to pay you for his expenses!!! Since he couldn't stand the climate, and we can't send money out of the island, even if I *could* earn enough."

The tragedy for Hall was exacerbated by the growing real-ization that Patricia's gender had played no small part in determining the role she played for the rest of her life. It was assumed, for instance, that Pat should look after her increas-ingly visually impaired brother. But if the situation had been reversed would George have sacrificed everything to look after Pat? Hall thought not.

Being aware of the day-to-day difficulties faced by his brother and sister back in Jamaica made it even harder for Hall to contemplate returning, for fear of being entrapped like they were. During one of their rare holidays in Jamaica in 1964–65, Hall realized with regret that his separation from his family and his mother in particular was accelerating. An off-the-cuff remark from Jessie, that she hoped the English wouldn't mistake him for one of those blacks or immigrants "over there", filled him with distaste. His mother followed that up with the startling statement that she thought "those immigrants should be pushed off the long end of a short cliff".

"I'd never ever called myself an immigrant before, but in

that moment I symbolically migrated,"[46] Hall explained, noting that until then he had maintained the fiction that he would return someday but in that decisive moment he realized he had indeed changed, had been transformed through his journey into a black immigrant.

During that period, the Trinidadian intellectual and economist Lloyd Best recalls calling on Hall for help with editing the first Jamaican edition of *New World Quarterly*, a journal produced and edited by a small group of intellectuals at the University of the West Indies. The two men had met on board the ship bringing Hall and Catherine to Jamaica for the first time since he had left. They had become friends and Hall was happy to share his considerable knowledge of the publishing business with Best and his friends.

The renowned Jamaican judge Hugh Small, who was urged by Hall to return to Jamaica after his studies in England, recalled seeing the Halls on one of their visits to Jamaica and being struck by the fact that Hall's hefty pile of reading material consisted mostly of women's periodicals. This was probably research Hall was conducting on a project titled "A Cure for Marriage" that constituted the lab work for a cultural studies book but was never written up for publication because the papers were lost.

Meanwhile, in 1972 Catherine started working at the Open University part-time, teaching history. Hall would put the children to bed while Catherine went to teach in the evenings.

Towards the end of the 1970s, feminist activism at the Birmingham Centre brought questions of gender to the forefront and forced Hall to realize that despite his fine-tuned awareness of the inequities of class and, increasingly, race, on the gender front he, like many other left-leaning men, had been curiously unresponsive and insensitive to the concerns of women.

Female scholars pointed out that the centre's "cutting-edge" research into subcultures and subcultural practices had failed to focus much on women and female subjectivity – the ten issues of *Working Papers in Cultural Studies* that the centre had published were unabashedly male-centred, with only four articles concerning women. In the opinion of Angela McRobbie, the most vocal of these critics, the research displayed an "unambiguously masculine prerogative".

In a landmark publication titled *Women Take Issue* (1978) authored by Angela McRobbie, Charlotte Brundson, Dorothy Hobson, Janice Winship and Rachel Harrison, who formed the Women's Studies Group, the male middle-class bias of the centre was critiqued. This feminist activism forced the research at the centre to be more inclusive and responsive to other "outsiders".

Hall was disheartened by the realization that despite being at the forefront of campaigning for disadvantaged and marginal groups' rights and despite the awareness he had gained through his marriage to a feminist, he had somehow, like all the other male scholars, overlooked the centrality of women to the project of the centre. Even though the "Cure for Marriage" project and his hiring of feminist lecturers during his tenure as head proved he had not entirely neglected questions of gender, Hall felt increasingly uncomfortable continuing as head of the centre and in 1979 made the momentous decision to leave Birmingham and accept the Open University's offer of heading its sociology department. In a later interview Hall represented this move with characteristic wit and humour: "So when the Vice Chancellor of the Open University said, 'But you've been in literature, you've been in cultural studies, are you willing to profess sociology?' I said, 'I'm willing to profess anything if you'll only give me a job'" (*Essential Essays* 2:272). He would spend the next eighteen years there developing and refining systems for the pedagogy of remote education.

British education, especially higher education, was enormously elitist in the 1950s. The small proportion of people going to university were mostly from public schools and from well-off families. After the war, ordinary English people started agitating for higher education. In 1969 the Open University, with roots in the egalitarianism of the Labour Party, opened the door to an intake with an entirely different social and class background. The Open University was founded without lecture halls (although it had a campus at Milton Keynes), using electronic media and books "to open up the ivory tower of knowledge".[47]

The Open University employed television and other broadcast media to deliver education at a distance, enabling working adults to acquire degrees. In addition to late-night lectures on BBC2, students were sent lecture course books, and their coursework was supervised. The Open University was more interdisciplinary than the average English university, allowing different academic interests – literary, cultural, sociological and historical – to be combined. With its embrace of pedagogical values such as interdisciplinarity and of lifelong learning, it was the ideal place for Hall, whose interest in and commitment to adult education had been kindled years earlier in Jamaica when he attended the 1950 Knox College summer school on community adult education.

In an unaired video interview conducted in London to mark Jamaica's fiftieth anniversary of independence in 2012, Hall expanded on the Open University, its function and origins, and how for him, working there was a particularly good fit:

> The Open University had a social purpose: it was egalitarian, it was widely distributing education, it was universalist, *everybody* should study, everybody *can* study if you put your mind to it, we can *all* improve our knowledge, we are *all* to be intelligent, we live in a democracy which depends on people making informed choices, how can you just educate an elite? So I was also attracted to the social purpose behind the Open University as well as its interdisciplinary character, and also the kind of students I taught because the majority of students I taught were older than twenty-one. Twenty-one-year-olds were going to the new universities but those who had missed out could still go to the Open University. So I taught more mature students. Mature in the sense of a lot of experience of life but not a lot of experience of studying academically. And I thought that's a rip-roaring educational challenge.

By then, television had made serious inroads into popular culture, reaching masses of people and facilitating the transition from class culture to mass culture. Hall had been one of the earliest to start teaching television and film, using the blockbuster movie *Doctor Zhivago* to talk about Stalinism, for instance, or westerns to discuss masculinity. In the early days, the 1950s and 1960s, television was viewed as a transparent, unbiased conveyor of reality, a misconception Hall and others found it important to dismantle.

Hall believed that the role of ideology in grasping and representing reality was at the crux of understanding how mass media messages are encoded by journalists and media entities and then decoded by mass audiences. "Reality" in his view was not self-evident but narratively constructed, by the stories journalists narrate about events and people. As he explained it, public communication between broadcasters and their audiences required two separate acts: the act of "encoding" the television or radio message, and the act of "decoding" and interpreting it. The encoding process was mostly performed by the professional broadcasting elites, with their own social formation, their own selective recruitment, their own social position, their own connections to and perspective on power, their own professional competences and routines, their own professional ideologies.

The decoding process was performed by the heterogeneous, complexly structured mass audiences, standing in their own relation to the unequal distribution of social, economic and cultural power, with their own connections to and perspectives on the system of power as a whole. Cultural power, according to Hall, included the differential acquisition by different strata of the population of the competence to speak, transmit, verbalize and comprehend – a form of power directly relevant to the capacity to communicate, and fundamentally shaped and distributed, in Western society, by the education system.

By the 1980s Hall's theory of encoding/decoding had become influential in media and communication studies and in the United States, where it was widely taken up without the scholars who used it realizing that he was, in the American context, black. It amused Hall no end that he was thus "decoded" in the wrong way because the concept of encoding/decoding did not explicitly reference race, which in the United States was widely felt to be the exclusive province of black scholars. However, if you had the historical and cultural background to decode it – the discursive frame – you would realize that what instigated Hall's deconstruction of media representations was the manner in which black and non-white subjects were often typecast by mainstream media. This was at the heart of the thesis of *Policing the Crisis*. It was in fact all about race and it came out of Hall's complicated relationship to Jamaica, only his theoretical reflections were encoded in such a way that it was possible for people all over the world, subjected to the same distortions in how they were represented, to decode his message and apply it to their own situations.

Being part of the Open University now allowed Hall to use television as a medium to communicate his thoughts and ideas to mass audiences in the United Kingdom because the prevailing preoccupation with books did not allow for new questions, arising from technological change, to be asked. "Television reorganizes the relationship between who is speaking and who is spoken to, and what a popular genre is, and how you touch popular emotions."[48] The Open University setup, where the lack of an academic background was *not* a barrier to entry, allowed Hall to transmit the cultural studies paradigm to a more popular level, in more accessible forms.

Naturally, teaching remotely required new processes and technologies. A former student and Open University colleague reminisced about Hall's extraordinary empathy and goodwill in mentoring junior colleagues like herself:

> Stuart enjoyed the seemingly endless work of drafting chapters and study guides, re-drafting and commenting on colleagues' chapters, discussing the choice of all words in assessment questions, debating the subtleties of the ideas we wanted to teach our students and expressing his high expectations of their capacities as mature adult learners. All this took place during intense bi-weekly day-long meetings over three years of course production to create fantastically honed course textbooks, which were widely admired – and extensively used! – outside the OU.[49]

The Open University proved to be an enormous success. By 1980 seventy thousand students had graduated and by 1998 it had produced two hundred thousand graduates.[50] Hall's weekly appearances on BBC2 made him a household figure and for black Britons, his electronic presence was even more significant. John Akomfrah, who years later would document Hall's life and work in *The Stuart Hall Project* and *Unfinished Conversation,* explained the impact of seeing Hall in that capacity:

Stuart Hall was a kind of rock star for us; a pop icon with brains whose very iconic presence on this most public of platforms – television – suggested all manner of "impossible possibilities". By just being there in our bedrooms and living rooms, he opened up pathways into that space that he has referred to as the place of "the unfinished conversation", that space in which the dialogue between us and the external world begins, that place of identity. With him and through him we began to ask the indispensable questions of that conversation: who are we, what are we and what could we become.

In those heady, mono-cultural days, he was one of the few people of colour we saw on television who wasn't crooning, dancing or running. I loved all the athletes and singers and dancers too but when you are a black teenage bookworm in seventies West London, let's just say a public intellectual of colour disseminating ideas on television offered other more immediate compensations.[51]

By the early 1980s, Hall's work had started to circulate in the United States. In 1983 he delivered a series of lectures at a teaching institute at the University of Illinois (Urbana-Champaign) and a conference immediately after, "Marxism and the Interpretation of Culture: Limits, Frontiers, Boundaries". Hall was part of a group of theorists and intellectuals on the cutting edge of cultural studies, communication, literary theory, film studies, anthropology and education who spoke at each venue to an audience of about five hundred young scholars. Gayatri Spivak, Fredric Jameson, Perry Anderson were some of the others. According to Lawrence Grossberg, one of Hall's students now teaching in the United States and one of the organizers of the events, the shape of cultural theory – its interpretation, directions, scholarships and teaching – in the United States at the time could be attributed to the institute and the conference and the influential book that came out of them. British cultural studies had officially arrived in the United States.

In 1994 Hall participated in a two-day conference at Princeton, a farewell to Cornel West, author of the book *Race Matters*, who was moving to Harvard. Over a thousand scholars were in attendance. Claire Alexander, who was there, described the recognition that greeted Hall when he spoke briefly:

> The conference was a veritable Who's Who of the African-American Academy – from West himself, to Toni Morrison, Manning Marable, Patricia Williams and Angela Davis. At the end of the opening panel, the floor was opened to questions and comments. The first speaker moved through the crowded audience to the microphone and quietly introduced himself – "Stuart Hall, The Open University". The room exploded into applause. It was the only time I have ever witnessed someone getting a standing ovation for simply saying their name. When I remarked on this later to Cornel West, he told me – "The thing you have to understand, Claire, is that we all grew up reading Stuart. We wouldn't be here without him. We all stand on his shoulders."[52]

Also in 1994 the Du Bois Institute for African and African American Research at Harvard University invited Hall to give the W.E.B. Du Bois Lectures, a trio of in-depth talks on race, ethnicity and nation, the "fateful triangle" of structuring categories of difference that persist in influencing social and political life. Henry Louis Gates Jr, then director of the institute, recalled that Hall eloquently taught how the old categories of difference failed to capture the complexity and blurriness of human life with its ever-recombining intersections and permutations of identities, histories and contexts: "He also made plain that, in pretending to represent anything close to pure boundaries between groups, those old categories carried with them histories of oppression, perpetuating dangerous group-think while reinforcing hierarchical notions of cultural difference. The slate needed to be wiped clean, and Stuart was holding the eraser."

By the mid-1990s Hall's work had become influential in shaping the field of racial and ethnic studies globally. He was now a foundational figure for scholars in Britain, the United States, the Caribbean, India, Hong Kong and beyond, redefining the parameters of race research and identity.

For almost two decades, Hall's work focused on "difference", or discursive models of difference, to understand how and why discourses of race, ethnicity and national belonging persisted in influencing the structure of social life. His 1988 article "New Ethnicities" looked at the signifier "black" and how it was re-signified in the United Kingdom by Afro-Caribbean and Asian people using it as an umbrella identity with which to counter the institutional racism and discrimination they encountered in Britain. By altering racial discourse itself through the expansion of the scope of black identity beyond the epidermal – difference – to the positional, conditional and conjunctural – *différance* – the ground was prepared for political and social change.

> Since cultural diversity is, increasingly, the fate of the modern world, and ethnic absolutism a regressive feature of late-modernity, the greatest danger now arises from forms of national and cultural identity – new or old – that attempt to secure their identity by adopting closed versions of "culture" or "community", and by the refusal to engage with the difficult problems that arise from trying to live with difference. The capacity to live with difference is, in my view, the coming question of the 21st century. New national movements that, in their struggle against old closures, reach for too closed, unitary, homogeneous and essentialist a reading of "culture" and "community", will have succeeded in overcoming one terrible historical hurdle only to fall at the second. (*Selected*, 281)

In 1987 the Hall family made another trip to Jamaica. Their daughter Becky, eager to explore her Jamaican heritage, was going to spend her gap year in Kingston working in the Cassava Piece area through the auspices of the Immaculate Conception Girls' School, where Hall's cousin Sister Maureen Clare was principal. Catherine had just finished the project that would result in her co-authored book with Leonore Davidoff, *Family Fortunes: Men and Women of the English Middle Class, 1780–1850*, and had time to spare but found the summer a difficult one, with the children both now at the angry adolescent stage and Hall conflicted about his relationship to Jamaica and where he belonged. After 1987 the trips to Jamaica became more frequent.

The following summer, while driving along the north coast

of Jamaica, near the town of Falmouth, the Halls passed a small village named Kettering. This seemingly mundane event proved to be life-changing for both husband and wife. Catherine Hall had been born in Kettering, Northampton-shire, in England and was struck by encountering its name-sake like this in faraway Jamaica. Her father, John Barrett, had been a Baptist minister. It was a moment of epiphany to now come upon Kettering in Jamaica with a Baptist chapel at the town centre. This chance encounter made Catherine realize that studying England and English history only through events and personalities based there was not enough. England was also formed by its relationships with its colonies: colony and metropole were inextricably linked. She would spend the next decade and more studying the inter-connections between the Baptist movement in Birmingham and Baptist missionaries such as William Knibb, whose name was emblazoned on the church in Kettering, Jamaica. Her 2002 book *Civilizing Subjects* was the culmination of this project and it would also reinvigorate Hall's intellectual work. Over the next few summers, the Halls drove all over Jamaica, up hilly, potholed roads, looking for the "free villages" established after abolition by the newly emancipated.

Catherine's work on the entanglement of the histories of Britain and Jamaica ignited Hall's interest in studying Englishness and identity, and the imbrication of people like himself – immigrants from Britain's former colonies – in the formation of English identity. Catherine's research had indirectly spurred his reconnection to Jamaica.

How to live with difference instead of suppressing it and

modifying it, how to manage the politics of difference without subjugating it, was the Gordian knot Hall was intent on unfastening. He deplored the "narrow little Englandism" increasingly in evidence, triggered "by the encroaching trauma of an emerging European identity" (*Selected*, 278). For Hall, it was necessary to systematically worry away at and unknot the exclusivity of English identity, to make manifest how it had been cobbled together from the various cultures and peoples it had colonized.

To disarticulate Englishness from whiteness and cultural homogeneity, Hall stressed the regular injections made into British culture by the foreign cultures Britain had colonized, and the culture that accompanied the wealth extracted from countries and civilizations beyond the shores of Britain. It was impossible to neatly extract the riches of a society without traces of its people and culture. Thus one *could* be black and British at the same time. It was a point Hall liked to stress: what is important in the formation of identity is not roots, biological, historical or otherwise, but the routes taken to get there:

> People like me who came to England in the 1950s have been there for centuries; symbolically, we have been there for centuries. I was coming home. I am the sugar at the bottom of the English cup of tea. I am the sweet tooth, the sugar plantations that rotted generations of English children's teeth. There are thousands of others beside me that are, you know, the cup of tea itself. Because they don't grow it in Lancashire, you know. Not a single tea plantation exists within the United Kingdom. This is the symbolization of English identity I mean,

what does anybody in the world know about an English person except that they can't get through the day without a cup of tea? Where does it come from? Ceylon – Sri Lanka, India. That is the outside history that is inside the history of the English.[53]

SEVEN

There is a widespread misconception in the Caribbean that cultural studies entails the analysis and critique of expressive or performative aspects of culture such as dance, drama, fiction, poetry and visual art. This is a narrow view of culture. For Hall, whose name is synonymous with this wide-ranging field of studies, the mission was intervening in politics and political culture, in representation, broadly speaking, with a view to altering the terms of engagement, whether it was higher education or the politics of citizenship. For Hall, cultural studies was a political project, a sustained but ever recalibrated reading of the contemporary conjuncture, whatever that might be.

Diaspora as a master concept had also become central to Hall's thought and mode of analysis. Not only was he a native of the Caribbean diaspora, the Caribbean itself was a diaspora. Hall's involvement in cultural studies was prompted by his attempts to think about Caribbean culture. What was Caribbean culture? What was the distinctive culture from which folks like himself were coming and what would Caribbean culture become in the diaspora? Would it stay the same, would it evolve, would it be destroyed by racism and the alien terrain it found itself in? What were the effects of double diasporization?

> The peoples in the Caribbean are all from somewhere else, the people who belonged here were stamped out by the Spanish conquistadores within a hundred years. Everybody else comes from somewhere else: the French, the Spanish, the Portuguese, the English, the Africans, the Lebanese, the Indians – you know, they're all from some other place so this is first a diaspora. Although there is a black diaspora in Britain, that is the diaspora of a diaspora, so I've been obliged to think about the culture of the black diaspora in Britain and the diasporized culture that has settled down and grown up in the Caribbean in diasporic terms. So it shaped my understanding of what culture is and how it works, yeah? The reason why I say culture is always a translation – there's no pure culture, it's always a translation – is because Jamaican culture is a translation of European and African and Indian cultures. And Jamaican culture in England is a translation of that translation composed out of African, European and Indian cultures in the Caribbean now further translated in relation to twenty-first century Britain and Europe. That is what culture is; it's not something which stands still, which never moves, which is intrinsic – born inside each of us which will never change, you know, we can never be something else. Culture is produced with each generation, we reproduce our own identities in the future rather than simply inherit them from the past.[54]

In 1991 Hall was given the opportunity for much closer engagement with the Caribbean when he was commissioned by BBC2 to produce a seven-part documentary series titled

Redemption Song on the region, presenting historically con-textualized vignettes on Jamaica, Haiti, Cuba, the Dominican Republic, Martinique, Trinidad and Tobago, and Guyana. In 1993 the BBC commissioned Hall to conduct an interview with Derek Walcott, who had just won the Nobel Prize.

Hall's commitment to writing and publishing continued through the 1990s. *Marxism Today*, the journal in which Hall had outlined his critique of Thatcherism, had ceased publishing in 1991. Ever one to appreciate the importance of a medium to continue developing the ideals and critical labour of the New Left, Hall, along with his Open University colleague and friend Doreen Massey and Michael Rustin, his lifelong comrade and friend, founded a new journal, *Soundings*, in 1995. From then until his death, *Soundings* became the publication through which Hall's writings and ideas were disseminated.

In 1996, for the first time, Hall was invited to speak at the University of the West Indies. There was a major conference on Caribbean culture in honour of Professor Rex Nettleford at Mona and Hall was one of six plenary speakers at the event. It was at this conference that Hall met David Scott, who was then at the Institute of Social and Economic Research. Scott interviewed Hall and the Trinidadian intellectual Lloyd Best for the inaugural issue of *Small Axe*, a journal of criticism that has become an institution, one very much influenced by Hall's own ideas on critical practice. Hall's relationship with Scott, an alumnus of Hall's old school, Jamaica College, was an important one, and by the time Hall passed away in 2014, Scott was widely acknowledged to be his intellectual heir.[55]

Hall's plenary address at the University of the West Indies, in which he was asked to ruminate on the future of Caribbean culture, focused on the subject of diaspora and the "double diasporization" of people like himself who lived in the diaspora of a diaspora.

The 1990s saw radical shifts take place both in Hall's life and focus. In 1997 he retired from the Open University and decided to spend his remaining years doing something that would not only intervene directly in the cultural politics of representation but would also bring him pleasure and present an enjoyable challenge. Visual culture and visual art were representational arenas which had always appealed to Hall and ones that were a logical progression from his decades-long focus on visual media such as film and television:

> There is something special about the image. I am slightly mystical about it. I do think that the ancients were right. That, you know, you take something from somebody when you take an image of them which is rather different from when you write about them. The image has a subliminal power; it always invites you to look longer and in places where your look is not always centred and your gaze does not always stop when you have seen enough. You always want to see a little bit more. I think the image is a very powerful communicator. But it is powerful also, I think, because it awakens emotions, strong emotions and feelings, subliminally; at the same time it is very open-ended in terms of its meaning. Images have a much wider connotative, associative reference, a much wider field of reference than words have.[56]

How artists and photographers were using visual media to

reconfigure their positions and identities in the diaspora were subjects that increasingly absorbed Hall's time and attention in the last quarter of his life. During this period Hall threw his energies into supporting a much younger set of artists, photographers and creatives in their struggle for visibility. The photographer and curator David Bailey was crucial in inducting Hall into the circuits of black image-making in Britain.

Since the 1970s and 1980s, Hall had been involved in recuperating the black image, both literally and figuratively. In 1979 and 1980 he was part of the production team of two anti-racist educational programmes: *It Ain't Half Racist, Mum* for the BBC, together with the Campaign against Racism in the Media, and *The Whites of Their Eyes* for the educational department of Thames Television.[57] Later, Hall met a film-maker who would become a close ally and friend – Isaac Julien, who drew him into the Sankofa Film and Video Collective, where Hall became even more immersed in film-making.

Hall found black photography, not only the documentary genre that was the focus of an earlier generation of image makers, but the constructed photographic images of a younger generation practising in the 1980s and 1990s, to be the visual counterpart of his work on identity and representation. "I was writing about identity and they were practising it. . . . It made me more alert to the way artistic work is exploratory space in which ideas work themselves out." Art was important, Hall said, because "such texts restore an imaginary fullness or plenitude, to set against the broken rubric of our past".[58]

The radicalism of the 1960s and militancy of the 1970s had given way to the conservatism and neoliberalism of the 1980s, with Thatcherism reconfiguring the field of black cultural politics, leading to a generation much more preoccupied with questions of black identity and self-representation.

There was a veritable explosion of creativity – in 1982 alone, there were ninety shows of work by black photographers and visual artists. Many black art galleries started in that period, in community centres, little places in Brixton. Much of the work asked such questions as Who am I? What is blackness? What is it to be black in Britain? Contrary to the realist, militant work of the previous generation, these artists used what Hall called the constructed image; they staged themselves, photographers included. Instead of seeing the photograph as a straightforward documentary record the next generation treated the photograph as a work of art, staging their otherness by using themselves – the black body, the black face, black beauty, black physique, black longing, black desire – as their subject matter, a kind of self-exploration through the visual arts.

The bold, spiritually charged and provocative images produced by artists such as Rotimi Fani-Kayode (which the latter termed "Yoruba modern art") recharged Hall with energy. He decided to lend his by now considerable influence and authority to this younger generation's fight for space and visibility. Two earlier generations had been denied a place at the table, their work routinely excluded from the canon of British art. The explosion of black creative work in and leading up to the 1980s put pressure on mainstream arts organizations – people started asking, Why isn't this work being shown? Why doesn't the Photographers' Gallery have any of these photographers who are producing work like crazy? Why had the Tate Gallery never exhibited even one member of the older generation, not even the venerable painter Frank Bowling, who, like fellow Guyanese artist Aubrey Williams, had never had a London retrospective despite his stellar work there?

A second generation of black artists also found their work excluded from mainstream British art institutions and because a lot of these were publicly funded, supported by the Arts Council for instance, it was possible to apply pressure on the arts institutions. The success of anti-racist activism and movements had sensitized the powers that be to the marginality of blacks in general in society and of black artists from the art institutions. So, gradually, organizations such as the London Arts Board and the Greater London Arts Council began to fund new institutions such as Autograph in 1988. An association of black photographers, with Fani-Kayode as its first chairman, Autograph was an artist-run organization trying to redefine itself as a professional body. At David Bailey's invitation Hall spoke at the launch of Autograph.

There was nothing narcissistic about the new focus on "territories of the self", Hall argued at the launch of Autograph's first exhibition, *Autoportraits*; rather, it was a significant move in the strategies and politics of black representation. The thinking behind the name "Autograph" was detailed in the blurb of the 2002 book *Different: A Historical Context* by Hall and Autograph's director Mark Sealy: "The book's main focus is the work of a selection of contemporary photographers who have used the image to explore and subvert the idea of 'black identity'. It charts their struggles to make the invisible visible, to open the third space in cultural representation, and to 'write' their experiences, their bodies and their subjectivities back into the frame from which they were excluded – a new kind of photographic 'writing-of-the-self' or *auto-graphy*."

In the mid-1980s a group had attempted to form Black Arts Centre in the old Roundhouse in London but failed. In 1994 Iniva – the Institute of International Visual Art – was founded with Hall as its chair. Iniva's first director, Gilane Tawadros, described the new institute as the culmination of efforts by artists playing the role of writers and curators in an effort to insert themselves into the critical sites of art history, art criticism and curatorship by broadening the frame of representation to accommodate perspectives on contemporary art and culture not premised uniquely on the intellectual and cultural priorities of the West.

A major feature of Iniva was the Stuart Hall Library, described as one of the leading UK libraries in the field of international visual art, with over four thousand exhibition catalogues, one thousand monographs – covering cultural, political, gender, and media studies – and over 140 periodicals. The library also held a substantial collection of monographs, catalogues, periodicals, DVDs, CDs, slides, and other media on visual arts and culture, with a focus on African, Asian and Latin American art, as well as British art from artists of diverse cultural backgrounds.[59]

Both Autograph and Iniva functioned initially as agencies,

rather than full-time galleries, because they represented a third generation of black British artists, who did not want to be ghettoized. As Hall put it, they did not want to have to go to the black arts gallery to show black work. They wanted to be part of Britain. Both organizations tried to challenge the mainstream to put work by black artists *in* the mainstream, to put the artists they represented in exhibitions of work in the existing galleries around the country. This was supplemented by producing books, by organizing talks, lectures, workshops, by reviewing the work of young artists and encouraging them; by doing small monographs which made their work more accessible; by producing the catalogues of shows so that after the show was finished there was something left that students could learn from. They acted as multipurpose agencies rather than traditional gallery spaces.

By the time Hall retired from the Open University in 1997, he was already chairman of the boards of Autograph and Iniva, now the Rivington Arts Centre. He had been president of the British Sociological Association from 1995 to 1997 but he was also enjoying working with younger artists and the constituencies around Iniva and Autograph, whose director Mark Sealy, along with Iniva's Gilane Tawadros, remained a close collaborator of Hall's. Hall joked that working with artists half his age was so rejuvenating, it was "like receiving a dose of monkey gland":[60] "When I retired in 1997 I thought, *don't* go on doing what you did before, get more involved in this stuff, which is what has happened. So since 1997 I've been giving more and more time to these two organizations and now to this project of building the arts centre."[61]

In the early 2000s it became apparent to both organizations that they did need their own exhibition space. Despite holding a number of successful exhibitions Hall and his collaborators realized that big mainstream galleries like the Serpentine, the Whitechapel, the Tate Modern and Tate Britain were not going to show edgy unknown black artists. They would show Chris Ofili and Steve McQueen because they had arrived and their well-established reputations ensured a market for their work, but in Hall's view this was not what Iniva and Autograph had aimed for.

Moreover, when these organizations finally put on shows in mainstream galleries, no one remembered the role they had played. After Iniva lobbied for years for an Aubrey Williams retrospective, finally persuading the Whitechapel Gallery to hold it, the show became known as *Whitechapel's* Aubrey Williams exhibition. No one remembered Iniva. "Who's Iniva?" they would ask, not realizing the organization's role in doing the research for the Aubrey Williams show, locating the paintings, selling Aubrey Williams to the Whitechapel Gallery, and producing the catalogue.

Hall and the management of Iniva decided that rather than remain invisible they would open a space to show the work of young black artists as well as artists from the Global South – a more culturally diverse set of visual artists than could be seen in the average London gallery.

"So we want a window in Britain for work from outside of Britain and we want a showcase in Britain for work produced in Britain, which doesn't get seen. So that's a project which I'm involved in now, which is Autograph and Iniva coming together, to launch the building. They've been given a Lottery grant of five million to build a new black and – you can't just say Black and Asian any longer because there are so many other migrant groups – but *culturally diverse* visual arts."[62]

Thus it was that Rivington Place came into being, with the intention of establishing the new venue as a major international visual arts centre in Shoreditch, London. The five-storey building was designed by star architect David Adjaye and opened to the public on 5 October 2007. It cost eight million pounds to complete and was the first publicly funded new-build international art gallery in London since the Hayward Gallery opened more than forty years earlier.

Adjaye, now more familiarly known as Sir David Adjaye, went on to design the Smithsonian National Museum of African American History and Culture, an architectural phenomenon that would have delighted Hall. Adjaye was one of the "new ethnics", the younger generation of artists and thinkers whose interaction with Hall had reinvigorated him in the 1990s and who in turn provided them with that rare beneficence – a hip one-man cheering squad not only willing to engage what they were doing but to enable it. Adjaye later said he would jokingly tell Hall that he was designing Rivington Place as a mask for him – an armour to wear in combat as Hall performed his stealthy, guerrilla intellectual manoeuvres.

Commenting on the younger "creatives" Hall surrounded himself with, Homi Bhabha, who had collaborated with Hall on numerous projects, observed, "The new ethnics named and nurtured by Stuart at the century's end – artists, filmmakers, dancers, photographers, critics, political organizers, writers – are embodiments of a long-cherished pedagogical and political project, going back to Birmingham, to establish a cohort of organic intellectuals."[63]

Hall's mission, therefore, was to not only *be* an intellectual but to transmit important ideas to others who were not necessarily intellectuals themselves. Being at the cutting edge of theoretical work was important to Hall, as Bruce Robbins pointed out, but also the work of turning other people into intellectuals. "The radical possibilities of intellectual work could be found in the ways it produced new intellectuals."[64]

EIGHT

D ecades of overwork and intense activity at home and work took their toll on Hall and by 1982, ill-health had set in. Never very robust, Hall found his life interrupted by frequent visits to the hospital. Now, with a diagnosis of end-stage renal failure, he was required to get dialysis three times a week but, ever open to new opportunities, Hall turned the visits into occasions to talk to the other patients, people he would never have met otherwise.

Animated discussions took place between the patients in the hospital waiting room about the latest episodes of *Neighbours* or *Coronation Street*, television shows that they all, Hall included, watched. Hall joked that "multicultural drift", a concept he had been talking about in relation to Britain, could be experienced live and in living colour at the dialysis unit of St Charles' Hospital where he went for his treatment. Increasingly, as he told Les Beck in an interview, it was a place where he did a lot of his thinking.

Multicultural drift was how Hall summarized the situation in Britain in the 1990s. This was not the same Britain he had arrived in in 1951. The population of Britain was far more diverse now, but it was the result of a gradual drift rather than a conscious movement. Multicultural drift was the result of slow, incremental change happening over the years, a passive revolution rather than the outcome of a ferocious battle for change. It was high time the United Kingdom started to revise policies designed on the premise of an almost exclusively white, English citizenry.

In 1998 Hall was invited to sit on the Runnymede Commission on the Future of Multi-Ethnic Britain. The commission was composed of people with a long record of intellectual and political engagement with race-related issues. Their recommendations (that British identity be delinked from its exclusive identification with Englishness and whiteness to reflect the myriad minority communities that are part of it and that the United Kingdom be redefined as "a community of communities" rather than a nation) were considered too radical, stirring up a storm of protest from right-wing media, who claimed the commission was trying to write Britain out of history. The commission had done no such thing in its report, wrote Hall in an article responding to the outcry but "perhaps unwisely, the report expected journalists to understand the distinction between 'racial' (as in a 'racial group') and 'racist' (as in 'a racist group')".[65]

New Labour, which came to office in 1997, had been a huge disappointment, a failure by the left to take on board Hall's insightful deconstruction of Thatcherism and the authoritarian populism that accompanied it. Instead of devising a counter-politics, New Labour had merely reformatted the conservative template of globalization and improved on it, resulting in what Hall considered the second phase of Thatcherism: Thatcherism v. 2. The main difference was that social democracy in its New Labour form was more successful than Thatcherism because it attended to the needs of those residually excluded – the poor. New Labour's solution was to adopt the new managerialism, to take the neoliberal capitalist model of globalization as a given, viewing it as something that had to be adjusted to and accommodated by adopting the ideology of the market.

Angela McRobbie, an alumna of the Centre for Contemporary Cultural Studies, Birmingham, now a major public intellectual herself, described the numerous occasions on which Hall and she sat on panels discussing the corrosive effect of the emerging neoliberalism, and how New Labour, through its vocal disavowal of left, feminist and anti-racist work as no longer relevant, "seemed to be attempting to engineer a disconnect, a disavowal of history through discounting the previous work of anti-racist groups and of alliances which had fought for equal opportunities and an end to workplace discrimination".[66]

By the early 2000s, according to McRobbie, New Labour was championing a new kind of black or Asian high achiever, the "top girls/boys" who could make good use of the meritocracy and make their way into the boardroom or legal chambers or indeed the House of Commons. The public relations machinery around New Labour sought out "feel-good" stories about successes in black and Asian business, not a radicalism which drew attention to racial violence, black urban poverty and unemployment, all of which supposedly belonged to the past. Instead, an echo chamber was created in which terms such as poverty and unemployment became synonymous with what was disapprovingly termed "dependency culture", depicting the poor as consumers of welfare benefits who weighed on the public purse.

The effect of market-driven mandates on the arts and culture were predictable, McRobbie suggests. The arrival of what she called "enterprise culture" compromised the quality of curriculum as well as pedagogy, as artists now had to spend more time promoting themselves, applying for grants and prizes, and finding sponsors in order to make work.

Iniva was headed by Gilane Tawadros in its first decade but after she left the organization in 2005, the board had difficulty replacing her and the institute started a slow but steady decline. Autograph, under the leadership of Mark Sealy, continued to thrive, its budget almost doubling, allowing it to assume management of Rivington Place.

All of this was disconcerting for Hall, who retired from the boards of both organizations in 2010. By then, despite having had hip replacement surgery, he was beginning to lose his mobility, first the ability to drive and then, gradually, the ability to walk. In 2011 Hall underwent a kidney transplant but was left weak and in pain afterwards, beginning a slow but steady decline. It was during this period that Hall, at the urging of friends and family, started writing his memoirs.

But before ill health started to immobilize him, the Halls spent many happy weekends at Catherine's cottage in Wivenhoe, Colchester. The adjoining cottage had been the studio of painter Francis Bacon and the Halls joked that the other side of their living room wall had been Bacon's easel. Hall's sense of mischief and humour were often evident, as when they were invited to dinner one evening in Colchester by mutual friends. One of the other guests, a young student from Germany named George, expressed mild annoyance at always being asked to bring Black Forest gateau with him just because he happened to come from the region. "Don't worry, young man," said Hall with a wink, "we all have our ethnic ghettoes/gateaux."

The Halls' home in West Hampstead was an inviting place full of photographs and artworks by the same group of artists Hall had bonded with in the 1980s and 1990s. Next to his chair in the living room stood a tall potted banana plant that seemed to thrive in that little oasis of domestic warmth. The Halls' many friends frequently dropped by and the couple often shared meals in the kitchen with close friends such as Paul Gilroy, Kobena Mercer, Julian Henriques and his wife Parminder Vir, assorted visitors from Jamaica, and colleagues. When the kitchen needed remodelling, Hall enlisted the services of a Jamaican cabinetmaker with a practice in London.

Life on the domestic front was immensely satisfying. The Hall children were grown up and Hall was happy that both, now adults, had found fulfilling work they enjoyed, Jess as a cinematographer in Hollywood (who worked on *Marley*, the 2012 biopic documenting the life of Bob Marley) and Becky as a child psychotherapist. The birth of Becky's son Noah, the Hall's first grandson, in 1998, was a source of great pride and joy. Hall and the young boy formed a close bond, with Noah calling his famous grandfather "Bear". When asked on the

BBC's *Desert Island Discs* programme in 2000 what luxury item he would like to take with him to the desert island, Hall responded: "The luxury I want is my grandson Noah. He's only fourteen months . . . we have long conversations but he doesn't yet speak." In 2001 Hall was presented with a second grandson, Ishaan, by his son Jess, who had married Radha Singh, from Rajasthan, India, a few years earlier.

In 1999 the University of the West Indies at Mona bestowed Hall with an honorary doctorate and Edward Baugh, who read the citation, noted that Hall had been a well-kept secret in Jamaica. In 2004 the Centre for Caribbean Thought held a conference in honour of Hall titled "Culture, Politics, Race and Diaspora: The Thought of Stuart Hall". Hall's response was self-deprecating as usual: "What is this strange object called *The Thought of Stuart Hall*? Who is this person that we've been discussing for two days? I sort of see him every now and again, I recognise some of him. I recognise some quotes but I don't recognise them all, and indeed I hope people will give me the references!" (*Essential Essays* 2:269).

In 2012 a huge celebration was organized at Rivington Place to celebrate Hall's eightieth birthday. Hall's close friends and associates from the various phases of his life gathered together in one spot, some of them meeting each other for the first time. Immobilized in a wheelchair, Hall later said it was somewhat frustrating as he would spot two friends in different corners of the room whom he wanted to introduce to each other, then realize with dismay that he was unable to just walk over and do so.

Upstairs in the auditorium, the first rushes of what would become *The Stuart Hall Project* were being screened by John Akomfrah. The celebration was also a moment for those whom Hall mentored to realize the breadth and strength of the web of relationships they belonged to, a network they could refer to and call on when needed.

In the waning years of his life, Hall's physical self may have begun disintegrating but his mind and critical faculties were as acute as ever. Asked if 9/11 and the wave of Muslim extremism following in its wake constituted a new conjuncture, Hall said that the politicization of Islam, as he preferred to call it, represented a new phase of the political formation set in motion by Thatcherism. It was difficult for people on the left, who were resolutely secular, to understand, because they had always dismissed religion: it was something that would/should recede in importance, they thought, and because of this: "Culture has taken its revenge on our failure to understand history. So, of course, in one sort of way I feel we'll never be the same again, and I think we may never be, but I wouldn't myself identify the conjunctural shift there [11 September 2001]. I identify it at another place."[67]

On 24 April 2013, less than a year before Hall died, he along with his Open University collaborator Doreen Massey and Michael Rustin, his brother-in-law and longtime partner in crime, launched *After Neoliberalism: The Kilburn Manifesto*. Over the following year the three pledged to examine different aspects of the current crisis and offer alternative approaches and demands in the hope of broadening the debate and opening a dialogue with a new generation shaped by different political experiences. It was a moment, they said, for challenging, not adapting to, neoliberalism's new reality.

Thus it was that almost up to the moment of his death, Hall continued attempting to intervene in the political conjuncture of the time, still reaching out and trying to forge alliances with a younger generation. He died on 10 February 2014, a week after turning eighty-two. The global outpouring of tributes and memorials that followed were a testament to the reach and influence of this great man.

Lawrence Grossberg summed up the valuable lessons he had learned from Hall: "He taught us how to think relationally and contexually, and therefore how to ask questions. He taught us how to think and even live with complexity and difference. He refused the all too easy binaries that theory and politics throw in our way – he described himself as a theoretical anti-humanist and a political humanist. Relations! Context! Complexity! Contingency! He inspired many of us with another vision of the intellectual life."[68]

In his book *Stuart Hall's Voice*, written as if its author was writing a letter to Hall, David Scott discusses the sonic and social qualities of Hall's voice, arguing that it was an integral component of his intellectual practice: "Resonance . . . is the proper name of your special register of intellectual presence. Your voice has a round, enveloping warmth and everyday modesty and cordiality about it . . . that has always had the demeanour of an invitation to join you in some conversation or other, that has always made me feel that it was *me* and not you who was saying something intelligent. Your voice, sonically, is like your fingerprint. It identifies you materially in a singular and unmistakable way."[69]

Homi Bhabha too remarked on the astonishing singularity of Hall's voice,

> redolent with a restrained music that I have heard amongst those who acquired the Queen's English in the colonies. It was a voice that was meticulous in its use of a language that had been "correctly" learnt at some distance from its native provenance, rather than naturally picked up; but it was also a voice that refused the prim protocols of "proper" English. Stuart's grain could not hold back the richly colored intonations of the Caribbean islands conveyed through the vowel music of Jamaican English with its extended Irish burr.[70]

The question of how Hall's intellectual interventions came to have such currency across the world was something many have tried to pin down. As McRobbie notes, he resolutely refused the "relentless and hubristic forms of self-promotion" practised by most academics eager to ascend the ranks of the now hegemonic "entrepreneurial university", practising instead an easily accessible and innovative style of scholarship. According to McRobbie this fostered large numbers of readers across the world and multiple translations of his work.[71] Hall influenced a wide range of disciplines beyond media and cultural studies, among them sociology and criminology, cultural anthropology, race and ethnicity studies, postcolonial studies, art history, and visual culture.

For Hall teaching was engaging in dialogue with people, having a conversation with them in which he shared his knowledge, rather than lecturing at students. It was what one observer called an attitude of "receptive generosity" in which listening was as important as speaking, receiving as important as giving:

> An ethics of receptive generosity . . . is an ethics that is committed not merely to giving to others, but to receiving from them as well. Such an ethics depends upon an attitude of vulnerable openness to learning from others, not merely masterfully teaching them – indeed, it is an ethics in which the former (learning) might be more important than the latter (teaching), or in which teaching is *itself* a way of learning, and learning a way of teaching.[72]

At heart, as Hall once said, he was a teacher; to teach was all this extraordinary man had ever wanted to do: "I could have lived a life of identifying myself with the English academic institution. I never have. I've taught in academic institutions. I honor the intellectual life. I love teaching and have always loved teaching. I've been an intellectual, but I've never been an academic" (*Personally Speaking*, 56). It might be said that Hall was genealogically disposed towards teaching by the tradition of teaching and education in his paternal family.

Hall never studied beyond the postgraduate level, but during his lifetime he was awarded twenty-nine honorary doctorates from universities around the world, and was courted by British politicians, who offered him a knighthood and a seat in the House of Lords. He turned both down. Since Hall's death the number of conferences and meetings held in his honour around the world has only proliferated.

Despite his global currency, Hall's death received little

acknowledgement in Jamaica, where neither radio nor television stations paused their broadcasts to take note of his passing. The *Gleaner*, Jamaica's main newspaper, editorialized the fact that "this intellectual treasure had neither popular nor official embrace in Jamaica" (12 February 2014):

> That not much has been made in Jamaica of the death this week of Stuart Hall should not, maybe, be surprising. After all, Professor Hall was 82 and had not lived here for 63 years.
>
> But our ignorance of Stuart Hall, at all levels of society, perhaps says more of national inattention to ideas and the people who generate them – especially the big ones. For as a thinker, Professor Hall would, in our view, be the equivalent to the likes of Usain Bolt.

The national inattention to ideas the editorial refers to is not unique to Jamaica; it is widely prevalent and possibly explains the reason for Hall's invisibility here. In a 2004 lecture, Hall said: "I think the world is fundamentally resistant to thought, I think it is resistant to 'theory'. I do not think it likes to be thought. I do not think it wants to be understood. So, inevitably, thinking is hard work, a kind of labor. It is not something that simply flows naturally from inside oneself" (*Essential Essays*, 2:304).

Ideas are often counterpoised to action, devalued as less substantial and therefore less capable of effecting change or affecting the "real" world than direct human action. The extent to which our actions are choreographed, driven even, by particular notions or ideas about the world and the "reality" thereof is not often acknowledged. To thinkers such as Hall, it was of paramount importance to recognize the power of ideology, systems of ideas and beliefs, in determining the meaning transmitted to objects, events and human interaction. "Myths can be as powerful in their ideological consequences as scientific truths," he famously said in his study on Rastafari.[73]

A stone, he was fond of saying, could be just that – a hard, rock-like object – but the very same stone could also be a boundary-marker or an art object, depending on the circuits it is inserted in and the additional meanings thereby ascribed to it. Based on how the stone is viewed it might be considered an object to move out of the way, an object that ought not to be moved at all lest a boundary be shifted, or a prized and valuable object to be guarded in a gallery or museum. There is therefore no one stable meaning attached to a stone, because depending on the discourse within which it is mobilized, it signifies or represents different things and commands different actions and reactions from its viewers.

Human society therefore is not straightforwardly the product of a universe of animate and inanimate objects whose meanings are fixed and easily available but a constellation of social constructions that are negotiated and agreed upon by different cultures. Cultures adhere because they agree on commonly held representations of the world; they also actively participate in constructing or constituting social systems based on their understanding of what things signify or mean.

Many of the things that Hall and his colleagues considered important in the 1960s and 1970s have become the new common sense today. When we look at the interactive nature of contemporary social media, the dialogic aspect of new media and digital communication in general, Hall's observations about the giving and taking of meaning, the coding and decoding embedded in circuits of communication come to mind. How power uses culture to bolster and sustain itself, and how culture can undo power, is essentially the crux of what animated his social analysis.

Even if Hall chose to live and work in Britain, he cleared a space for Jamaicans like himself and others from the Caribbean, and beyond them for migrants from all over the world, to not only make lives in Britain but in so doing to irrevocably transform the mother culture. There is much to be gained by adopting Hall's approach to teaching and learning, his humility and appreciation for intellectual work, and his non-competitive, collaborative approach to life and learning.

In the final analysis, David Scott's tribute to Hall, given at the memorial service in his honour at The Light, the Quaker place of worship in London, sums up the situation and the man best:

> Jamaica scarcely recognized Stuart, maybe no one should be surprised by this. He certainly wasn't. Because he understood that part of what makes Jamaica enviably, unsettlingly Jamaica, part of what draws from us a grudging admiration, is precisely its scornfully prideful soul, its insouciant indifference even to its own, its willful, sometimes self-destructive, don't care attitude . . . its proverbial ethic of not begging anyone a glass of ice water. Stuart, I think, would have been the first to salute the

defiant principle of this moral posture as an invaluable inheritance from the bitter past, it was in a very special way his inheritance too, in fact in that instinct for independent-mindedness, for finding his own way, his own idiom of dissent and refusal, in his way of being done, finished with exhausted phases of his life, we recognize something familiar, something that made him, to paraphrase C.L.R. James – of Jamaica, Jamaican.

During his lifetime this unusual Jamaican was not interested in personal fame or gain, spurning prestigious awards and the lure of individual authorship, preferring instead the live and direct action of intervening in political and cultural conjunctures. The seeds of such interventions fell on fertile ground, attracting young minds looking to move beyond the Manichean dichotomies of modern discourse. Thus Hall's ideas and his reputation spread by dispersal, quietly but persistently subverting dominant ideologies in much the same way as diasporas – his favoured analytic object in later years – subverted imperial custom and tradition. The notion of dissemination, of scattering knowledge far and wide, was crucial to this innovative intellectual's thinking and practice. "The seed has gone out," as Hall might have said, and the world would never be the same again.

NOTES

1. Hall, *Selected Political Writings*, 277. This and all book-length works by Hall are hereafter cited in the text using short titles.
2. In the early twentieth century the United Fruit Company was the centre of the banana industry in Jamaica, bananas being the main crop to supplant sugar as a staple export.
3. On their visits to Kingston, the Halls always stayed at the Convent, in graceful buildings built a century or more ago, surrounded by golfing greens, where they were able to spend time with Sister Maureen Clare. Catherine continues to stay there to this day.
4. In the 1991 BBC documentary film series on the Caribbean, *Redemption Song*, featuring Hall, he can be seen visiting the schoolroom and talking with his aunt Gerry, who was by then a centenarian.
5. Much of the familial information in these early chapters is drawn from Hall's posthumously published memoir *Familiar Stranger* and a transcript of the DVD interview *Personally Speaking*.
6. This was a fact Hall encountered through a website to which Catherine had contributed, Legacies of British Slave-Ownership (https://www.ucl.ac.uk/lbs/), a database containing the identity of thousands of slaveholders in the British colonies at the time slavery ended and, second, many of the estates in the British Caribbean colonies with details about these families.

7. Henriques, *Family and Colour*, 44–45.

8. Levy, *Hash and Roast Beef*, 11.

9. Personal reminiscence of sociologist John Maxwell, a stalwart at the University of the West Indies for many years.

10. Hall, "Formation", 489–90.

11. This and the following quotes are from unpublished papers in the personal archives at the Hall home at 10 Ulysses Road, London. I am indebted to Catherine Hall for giving me access to this material.

12. Padmore, "Federation", 63.

13. Leavis, *Great Tradition*, 11.

14. Hall, "Conversation", n.p.

15. Francis, "Travelling Miles", 145.

16. This passage and several others in this chapter are quoted from unpublished fragments of fiction that Hall wrote in his student days at Oxford, obtained from his personal archives.

17. Cliff, *If I Could*, 89.

18. This fictional fragment and the quotes following in the rest of this chapter come from unpublished documents in Hall's personal archives.

19. Hall, "Caribbean Culture", 33.

20. This and other early essays on the Caribbean remain unpublished and were obtained from Hall's personal archives.

21. Philip, "Battle", n.p.

22. Hall, "Politics", 149.

23. Hall, "The New Conservatism and the Old", *Universities and Left Review* 1, no. 1 (1957): 21–23.

24. Hall, "Life and Times".

25. So important did his relationship with the Hastons become that in 1964 Hall's wedding was held at the Haston home in Clapton. Much later the Jamaican sociologist Orlando Patterson would live there as well.

26. Hall, "At Home", 671.

27. Hall, "Absolute Beginnings", 20.
28. Raphael Samuel, a creative historian and intellectual, became a significant person in Hall's life. Samuel was instrumental in founding *History Workshop*, an innovative cultural historical journal Catherine Hall would later become an editor of.
29. Hall, "Sense of Classlessness", 26.
30. Ibid.
31. Williams, *Culture and Society*, 324.
32. Better known today as the Notting Hill Riots.
33. Hall, "Life and Times", n.p.
34. Hall, "Absolute Beginnings", 17–25. Michael de Freitas emigrated to London in 1957 from Trinidad. He renamed himself Michael X, styling his politics on the Black Power movement in the United States. In 1969 he founded the Racial Adjustment Action Society and became the self-appointed leader of a Black Power commune on Holloway Road, North London, called the Black House. John Lennon, a huge supporter of the charismatic Michael X, bailed him out of jail on one occasion.
35. Hall, "Television", 2.
36. The history of the Centre for Contemporary Cultural Studies reflects its imbrication with the literary history of the day, in particular, a landmark ruling against literary censorship. Richard Hoggart, who founded the Birmingham Centre in 1964 as an outcrop of the English department at the University of Birmingham, had joined Birmingham University as professor of English. When the university warned him it had no money to pay for the centre, funds were supplied by an unlikely source. In 1960 Hoggart had testified on behalf of Penguin Books, playing a starring role in the highly publicized obscenity trial against the publisher regarding its unexpurgated publication of *Lady Chatterley's Lover* by D.H. Lawrence. Penguin was acquitted and Hoggart persuaded the head of Penguin, Sir Allen Lane, to fund a research centre. Lane gave Hoggart a few thousand pounds a

year, which he wrote off against taxes, and it was this money that Hoggart used to hire Hall to establish cultural studies at the centre, while he remained professor of English.

37. Hall, "Conversation".

38. Hilton and Connell, "Stuart Hall", n.p.

39. Hall, "On Postmodernism", 59.

40. Born in Sardinia in 1860, Gramsci became a socialist, championing the rights of Sardinian and then Italian workers. A formidable and influential writer, he started a weekly newspaper in Turin and in 1921 became a founding member of the Communist Party of Italy. In 1926 he was arrested by Mussolini's fascist police and sent to prison. At his trial the prosecutor allegedly said, "For twenty years we must stop this brain from functioning." He was duly sentenced to twenty years in prison, where he wrote his hugely influential *Prison Notebooks*. Despite being written in obtuse language designed to frustrate the prison censors, in the twenty-first century the *Notebooks* continue to have relevance for organizations, leaders and theorists across a wide political spectrum.

41. Dawson, "Policing".

42. Jensen, "Classic Book", n.p.

43. Oudenampsen, "Revisiting".

44. Dworkin, *Cultural Marxism*.

45. C. Hall, *Civilising Subjects*, 4.

46. Hall, "Conversation", n.p.

47. Saldanha, "Power Geometry".

48. Hall, "Politics", 148.

49. Evans, "Stuart Hall".

50. Saldanha, "Power Geometry".

51. *Stuart Hall Project*, DVD booklet.

52. Alexander, introduction, n.p.

53. Hall, "Old and New", 48–49.

54. Hall, "Ironies", 66–67.

55. David Scott's short sojourn as a researcher/lecturer at the University of the West Indies (1996–99) is reflective of a prevalent indifference at that institution to *Small Axe* and its project of reviving an oppositional and critical enterprise. Indirectly this also indexes a lack of interest in the kinds of ideas associated with Hall. There was a similar coolness towards the ideas and intellectual practices of cultural scholars such as Erna Brodber and Kamau Brathwaite. In 1999 Scott migrated to the United States, taking *Small Axe* with him, where it has become a standard-bearer of critical reflection by Caribbean scholars, artists and writers.

56. Hall, "Work", 11.

57. von Rosenberg, "Stuart Hall", 66.

58. Hall, "Identity", n.p.

59. https://www.contemporaryand.com/publication/inside-the-library -ii-stuart-hall-library-iniva-london/.

60. Hall, "At Home".

61. Hall, "Ironies", 64.

62. Ibid., 63.

63. Bhabha, "Beginnings", n.p.

64. Robbins, "Starting Point", n.p.

65. Stuart Hall, "A Question of Identity (II)", *Guardian*, 15 October 2000. https://www.theguardian.com/uk/2000/oct/15/britishid entity.comment1.

66. McRobbie, "Stuart Hall", 671.

67. Hall, "Interview", n.p.

68. Grossberg, "Rage", n.p.

69. Scott, *Stuart Hall's Voice*, 50.

70. Bhabha, "Beginnings", n.p.

71. McRobbie, "Stuart Hall".

72. Scott, *Stuart Hall's Voice*, 117.

73. Hall, "Religious Ideologies", 271.

BIBLIOGRAPHY

Alexander, Claire. Introduction. *Stuart Hall and "Race"*, edited by
    Claire Alexander. London: Routledge, 2009. https://doi.org/10
    .1080/09502380902950914.

Bhabha, Homi. "The Beginnings of Their Own Enunciations: Stuart
    Hall and the Work of Culture". *Critical Inquiry*. https://critical
    inquiry.uchicago.edu/homi_k._bhabha_on_stuart_hall.

Cliff, Michelle. *If I Could Write This in Fire*. Minneapolis: University
    of Minnesota Press, 2009.

Dawson, Ashley. "Policing the Crisis". *Counterpunch*. 11 August 2011.
    https://www.counterpunch.org/2011/08/11/policing-the-crisis/.

Dworkin, Dennis. *Cultural Marxism in Postwar Britain: History, the
    New Left, and the Origins of Cultural Studies*. Durham, NC: Duke
    University Press.

Evans, Jessica. "Stuart Hall: An OU Perspective". 14 February 2014.
    https://www.open.edu/openlearn/society/politics-policy-people
    /stuart-hall-ou-perspective.

Francis, Donette. "Travelling Miles: Jazz in the Making of a West In-
    dian Intellectual". In *Caribbean Culture: Soundings on Kamau Brath-
    waite*, edited by Annie Paul, 142–51. Kingston: University of the
    West Indies Press, 2007.

Grossberg, Lawrence. "Rage Against the Dying of a Light: Stuart Hall
    (1932–2014)". *Truthout*. 15 February 2014. http://www.truth
    -out.org/opinion/item/21895-rage-against-the-dying-of-a-light
    -stuart-hall-1932-2014.

Hall, Catherine. *Civilising Subjects: Metropole and Colony in the English Imagination, 1830–1867.* Cambridge: Polity Press, 2002.

Hall, Stuart. "Absolute Beginnings: Reflections on the Secondary Modern Generation". *Universities and Left Review* 7 (Autumn 1959): 17–25.

———. "Caribbean Culture: Future Trends". *Caribbean Quarterly* 43, nos. 1–2 (March-June 1997): 25–33.

———. "A Conversation with Stuart Hall". *Journal of the International Institute* 7, no. 1 (Fall 1999). http://hdl.handle.net/2027/spo .4750978.0007.107.

———. *Cultural Studies 1983. A Theoretical History.* Edited by Jennifer Daryl Slack and Lawrence Grossberg. Durham, NC: Duke University Press, 2016.

———. *Familiar Stranger: A Life between Two Islands.* Durham, NC: Duke University Press, 2017.

———. "Formation of a Diasporic Intellectual: An Interview with Stuart Hall". By Kuan-Hsing Chen. In *Stuart Hall: Critical Dialogues in Cultural Studies,* edited by Kuan-Hsing Chen and David Morley, 484–503. London: Routledge, 1996.

———. "Identity and the Black Photographic Image". *Ten.8* 2, no. 3 (Spring 1992): 24–31.

———. "Interview with Caryl Phillips". *BOMB*, no. 58 (Winter 1997). https://bombmagazine.org/articles/stuart-hall/.

———. "The Ironies of History: An Interview with Annie Paul". *Ideaz* 3, nos. 1–2 (2004): 53–80.

———. "Life and Times of the New Left". *New Left Review* 61 (January–February 2010). https://newleftreview.org/issues/II61/articles /stuart-hall-life-and-times-of-the-first-new-left.

———. "Old and New Identities, Old and New Ethnicities". In *Culture, Globalization and the World System,* ed. Anthony King, 41–68. London: Macmillan, 1991.

———. *Personally Speaking: A Long Conversation with Stuart Hall.* By

Michael Dibb, Cheli Duran and Maya Jaggi. Northampton, MA: Media Education Foundation Collection, 2014. [Film and transcript.] http://ed.kanopystreaming.com/node/84657.

———. *Policing the Crisis: Mugging, the State, and Law and Order.* London: Macmillan, 1978.

———. "Politics, Contingency, Strategy: An Interview with Stuart Hall by David Scott". *Small Axe*, no. 1 (February 1997): 141–59.

———. "On Postmodernism and Articulation: An Interview with Stuart Hall". *Journal of Communication Inquiry* 10, no. 2 (1986): 45–60.

———. "Religious Ideologies and Social Movements in Jamaica". In *Religion and Ideology*, edited by R. Bocock and K. Thompson, 269–97. Manchester, UK: Manchester University Press, 1985.

———. *Selected Political Writings.* Durham, NC: Duke University Press, 2017.

———. "A Sense of Classlessness". *Universities and Left Review* 5 (Autumn 1958): 26–32.

———. *Stuart Hall: Essential Essays.* Volume 2, *Identity and Diaspora.* Edited by David Morley. Durham, NC: Duke University Press, 2018.

———. "Television as a Medium and Its Relation to Culture". Centre for Contemporary Cultural Studies stencilled occasional papers, 1975.

———. "The Work of Art in the Electronic Age: Interviews with Jean Baudrillard, Stuart Hall, and Paul Virilio". *Block*, no. 14 (Autumn 1988): 11–14.

Hall, Stuart, and Mark Sealy. 2001. *Different.* London: Phaidon.

Henriques, Fernando. *Family and Colour in Jamaica.* London: Eyre and Spottiswoode, 1953.

Hilton, Matthew, and Kieran Connell. "Stuart Hall". N.d. https://www.birmingham.ac.uk/research/perspective/stuart-hallhilton-and-connell.aspx.

Jensen, Tracey. "Classic Book: *Policing the Crisis*". 1 February 2014. https://www.redpepper.org.uk/classic-book-policing-the-crisis/.

Leavis, F.R. *The Great Tradition: George Eliot, Henry James, Joseph Conrad.* London: Chatto and Windus, 1960.

Levy, Charles. *Hash and Roast Beef.* Kingston: Griffin, 2013.

McRobbie, Angela. "Stuart Hall: Art and the Politics of Black Cultural Production". *South Atlantic Quarterly* 115, no. 4 (2016): 665–83.

Oudenampsen, Merijn. "Revisiting *Policing the Crisis*". 7 May 2014. https://merijnoudenampsen.org/2014/05/07/revisiting-policing -the-crisis/.

Padmore, Overand. "Federation: The Demise of an Idea". *Social and Economic Studies* 48, no. 4 (December 1999): 21–65.

Philip, Bruno. "Battle against Oblivion: The Defeat That Ended French Colonial Rule in Vietnam". *Guardian*, 1 July 2014. https://www .theguardian.com/world/2014/jul/01/dien-bien-phu-battle-france -vietnam-indochina-war.

Robbins, Bruce. "A Starting Point for Politics: The Radical Life and Times of Stuart Hall". *Nation*. 27 October 2016. https://www .thenation.com/article/the-radical-life-of-stuart-hall/.

Saldanha, Arun. "Power Geometry as Philosophy of Space". In *Spatial Politics: Essays for Doreen Massey*, edited by David Featherstone and Joe Painter, 44–55. London: Wiley.

Scott, David. *Stuart Hall's Voice: Intimations of an Ethics of Receptive Generosity.* Durham, NC: Duke University Press, 2017.

von Rosenberg, Ingrid. "Stuart Hall and Black British Art" in "Culture, Power and Identity: The Theoretical Legacy of Stuart Hall", edited by Florian Cord and Gerold Sedlmayr. Special issue, *Coils of the Serpent*, no. 3 (2018): 62–87.

Williams, Raymond. *Culture and Society, 1780–1950.* London: Chatto and Windus, 1958.

ACKNOWLEDGEMENTS

I first met Stuart Hall in 1996 during the Rex Nettleford Conference at the University of the West Indies in Jamaica. We hit it off immediately, remaining great friends until his death in 2014. During that period, I would route every trip through London, if possible, to facilitate meetings with my, by now, informal mentor. We would take in an Isaac Julien opening or the latest exhibition at the Serpentine, invariably followed by a meal, or meet for tea at Stuart's favourite hotel, the Russell Square. In between, we stayed in touch by phone, with Stuart eager to hear about the latest ructions in the Jamaican art world. After he became less mobile, we met at the Halls' Ulysses Road home, where Stuart would cook and serve a simple meal himself. We bonded over our common interest in media and visual art (I was then writing a column for the *Jamaica Herald* and involved in starting the new journal *Small Axe*), and Stuart opened many doors for me over the course of our friendship. This book is a small attempt at reciprocating Hall's generosity by ensuring that readers in the Caribbean learn more about this remarkable man whose warmth and accessibility far belied his global stature.

Linda Speth, the former director of the University of the West Indies Press, must be thanked profusely for initiating the Caribbean Biography Series before she retired and for inviting me to write this biography. She gave me an opportunity I will always appreciate. Thanks also to Sister Maureen Clare of Immaculate Conception

Convent, who willingly shared memories of her cousin Stuart in his youth. Thanks especially to Catherine Hall, whose friendship has also meant a lot to me over the years. She generously gave me access to the personal archives retained by the family (the bulk of Stuart Hall's archives having gone to the Cadbury Research Library at the University of Birmingham). These items of private correspondence and unpublished writings, portions of which are being published for the first time in this biography, led to critical insights for me and proved vital in resurrecting Stuart Hall's much less known early years in Jamaica.

Shivaun Hearne provided invaluable advice about the final shaping of the book, which helped to bring to completion four years of work. Tejaswini Niranjana is the one from whom I first heard about Stuart Hall and cultural studies, so I must thank her. Thanks also to my personal network of friends and family, who have sustained me all these years and enabled my writing life. Heather Gallimore, Anthony Miller, Mikie Bennett, Richard "Dingo" Dingwall, Susanne Fredricks – thanks for being there. Deborah Thomas, Michaeline Crichlow, Kumi Naidoo, Achal Prabhala, Sheri Markose, Julian Henriques, Yaba Badoe, Anu Lakhan, Faith Smith, Donnette Francis have all been great interlocutors over the years, physical distance notwithstanding. For introducing me to Stuart Hall all those years ago and nurturing my early writing, I'm grateful to David Scott.

And finally, let me acknowledge my daughter-in-law, Jonessa Wright Baker, and her wonderful children, Cafu and Zoii, who have enriched my life immensely, and of course my sun, Varun Baker.

www.ingramcontent.com/pod-product-compliance
Lightning Source LLC
Chambersburg PA
CBHW031850090426
42741CB00005B/437